I0154467

PEORIA STORIES

WEST BLUFF
CHRISTIAN
CHAPEL

PEORIA STORIES

TALES FROM THE ILLINOIS HEARTLAND

KEN ZURSKI

AUTHOR OF *THE WRECK OF THE COLUMBIA*

Peoria Stories © Copyright 2014, Ken Zurski

All rights reserved. No part of this book may be used or reproduced in any manner whatsoever without written permission from the publisher, except in the case of brief quotations in critical articles and reviews.

First Edition   ISBN 13: 978-1-937484-23-1

AMIKA PRESS   466 Central AVE #23 Northfield IL 60093   847 920 8084 info@amikapress.com   Available for purchase on amikapress.com

Edited by John Manos.

Front cover photograph courtesy the Wheels O' Time Museum, Dunlap, IL. Back cover photographs courtesy *Peoria Daily-Transcript, Peoria Journal, Peoria Herald, Peoria Herald-Transcript, Peoria Journal-Transcript,* & *Peoria Star.* Title photograph courtesy the Peoria Historical Society Collection/ Bradley University Library. Author photograph by Ken Zurski. Designed & typeset by Sarah Koz. Body in Walbaum, designed by Walbaum Justus Erich in 1800, digitized by František Štorm in 2010. Titles in Modesto Condensed Light, designed by Jim Parkinson in 2000. Thanks to Nathan Matteson.

FOR MY WIFE, CONNIE,
WHO BROUGHT ME HERE.

"History is a faithful narration of facts of yesterday, registered upon time's leaf today, to be turned over tomorrow." —Anonymous

WITHIN THESE pages are true stories. Some have been forgotten, others have been retold, and some, in my opinion, needed more telling. They are narrative snapshots of the past with an emphasis on the central part of Illinois, specifically Peoria and its immediate region. In these stories you will meet many interesting characters, some you may recognize, and some you may not. I hope you find their lives and adventures as fascinating as I do. Much of the information used for historical backgrounds is taken from a wide-ranging resource of books, newspapers, journals, letters, and other related material. Sources are included in the end notes. In many instances, a combination of sources was used to better narrate the story. No quoted words have been altered in any way, and some descriptions have been reclaimed from contemporaneous written material. Any speculation by other authors is noted as such.

CONTENTS

AN AFFECTIONATE FAREWELL

Abraham Lincoln made only occasional stops in Peoria, even to visit. This was not unusual for Lincoln, who hardly visited anyone, anywhere, except his stepmother in Charleston, Illinois, and even that was rare. This does not mean, however, that Lincoln didn't travel. As a lawyer in the eighth judicial district, he frequented many cities in Illinois, but almost always to cover cases. Lincoln would make the best of his stays, for sure, oftentimes enjoying the company and establishments in each town before moving on to the next, the linked sequence of locations called a circuit. Many cities in Illinois honor the time, however briefly, the future president spent in their communities. He undoubtedly left a large footprint in the state. Statues and plaques adorn many city parks and courthouses, and for generations local historians and writers have kept the tales of Lincoln's sojourns in their small towns vividly alive. If he wasn't there for business, the stories generally go, he was just traveling through. But he was there. Peoria was not part of the eighth district, so Lincoln's time spent in the city was limited. Just the same, Lincoln is closely tied with Peoria for one singular day—and one speech. The story that follows explains why he was in Peoria that day and why it was such an important event. Despite being born in Kentucky, Lincoln came to Illinois as a young man. So Illinois is and always has been considered Lincoln's home state. He spent most of his adult life in Illinois. It's where he met his wife, started a family, ran a business, and buried his second born son. So when he left to become president, Lincoln said a heartfelt goodbye to the people of his beloved Illinois. He would never return. And his rise to the White House, some would argue, began on a street corner in Peoria.

"THIS IS my literary bureau," said president-elect Abraham Lincoln as he handed a "well-filled" satchel to Mrs. Elizabeth Grimsley, daughter of Dr. John Todd, who happened to be the uncle of Lincoln's wife, Mary.

It was early February 1861, and Lincoln had stopped by the doctor's home (said to be one of the largest in Springfield) just days before traveling by train to Washington, D.C., where he would begin his first term as President of the United States. He asked Mrs. Grimsley to keep the bureau in her charge. It contained writings and lectures he hoped to save; his plan was to reclaim the bureau if he returned to Springfield. "But if not," Lincoln said, "please dispose of its contents as deemed proper."

A friend of Lincoln's, Dr. Samuel Houston Melvin, was also present that day. He remembered: "A tone of indescribable sadness was noted in the later part of [Lincoln's] sentence."

Melvin's concerns for his friend were warranted. A few days earlier, Lincoln had shown Melvin several letters "threatening [Lincoln's] life." Some predicted that Lincoln would never live to see his inauguration day.

"It was apparent to me that the threats were making an impression on his mind," Melvin continued, "although he tried to laugh the matter off." The literary bureau, not the threatening letters, Lincoln insisted, was of more importance.

While the threats on Lincoln's life were alarming, especially to his closest confidants, they weren't surprising. In 1861 Lincoln was, as one writer put it, "the most feared and most famous person in America." He was also the most vulnerable. Even the celebratory train ride to Washington was getting notice. After suspecting a possible ambush near Baltimore, a plan was crafted by the Pinkerton Detective Agency to keep the president-elect off the inaugural train—or at least concealed by a disguise—during the stretches deemed most susceptible to marauders or, worse yet, assassins. Lincoln would eventually go along with the plan, but no trouble occurred, or as Pinkerton would like to claim, was "thwarted" before it occurred.

Slavery was the inescapable issue during the fall of 1860, and Lincoln was the intentional instigator. The recently failed Senate candidate, whom many believed would never make it back to Washington, was now seen as America's savior by those who supported his views on slavery and by slaves themselves who took a sudden interest in politics. Lincoln, they were told, although many did not know him by sight, "would set them free." Even southern newspapers noted the attention of slaves who lingered near courthouse squares and eavesdropped at local hustings, just to hear what the orators had to say.

On the other side were the plantation owners whose livelihoods were being threatened by a man they hardly knew. Lincoln had remained mostly out of politics after his single term in Congress ended in 1849, but as a private citizen he was asked to speak at several events and outings. People took notice. Soon there was a grassroots effort—fueled mostly by journalists—to consider the lanky lawyer from Illinois a potential nominee for president. When one reporter asked Lincoln about such a candidacy, he remarked, "I must in candor say I do not think myself fit for Presidency." But it was not a choice. Lincoln, a Whig Party favorite, was the spokesman for a contentious debate. Although many still knew little about him, his views on slavery were resonating across the land. His candidacy for president became unavoidable.

In addition, an outpouring of criticism, especially from the South, was inevitable.

Lincoln's actions could hardly be blamed for the Southern anger that was growing against him. In fact, the folksy lawyer mostly remained in Springfield during the 1860 campaign, continuing his law practice from the safety and comfort of his home office. At the time, this was not an uncommon practice for presidential hopefuls who resisted the unpredictability of stump appearances in favor of quiet dignity and respect. Not one public statement was released during this time. "Refer to my published speeches and debates," Lincoln would tell the eager reporters who often made long and frustrating trips to Springfield see him.

But the campaign of 1860 was changing in ways that Lincoln the man was not. Lincoln's onetime Senate rival, fellow Illinois politician and now presidential opponent, Stephen Douglas, jumped at the chance to entertain and enlighten an audience with his views. On a trip from Illinois to upstate New York to see his aging mother, Douglas made several unplanned stops at railway stations along the way, stirring up crowds who demanded a speech. Douglas was happy to oblige the excited throngs, but the trip itself became a national joke—taking nearly two full months with detoured stops through New England, Pennsylvania, and Maryland. Even Douglas' intent was questioned. Did he really plan to see his mother? No one was really quite sure.

Lincoln held no grudge against Douglas or his tactics. To Lincoln, they simply experienced a difference of opinion in most matters. But as campaigners, they were literally miles apart. Lincoln had nothing to hide, he said, and instead let his long list of public orations suffice. These included a series of statewide debates with Douglas preceded by two speeches in Springfield and Peoria, where Lincoln directly challenged those on both sides of the slavery issue. "Wherever slavery is," he told the crowd on the state fairgrounds in Springfield, "it has been first introduced without law." The speech in Peoria was similar to the one in Springfield, but it is better remembered because Lincoln wrote it out for publication. Called the *Peoria Speech,* many historians widely regard it as Lincoln's finest moment, one that "changed the history of the United States."

LINCOLN SPOKE plainly that day in Peoria, his remarks grounded in historical research, holding forth against slavery and the moral judgment of men who are "created equal" by law. As he stated it: "Near eighty years ago we began by declaring all men are created equal, but now from that beginning we have run down to the other declaration, that for some men to enslave others is a 'sacred right of self-government.'

"These principles," he declared, "cannot stand together."

The speech put Lincoln in the center of the national debate over slavery and, more importantly, it put him back in politics. The one-term congressman from Illinois, virtually out of the public eye for nearly five years, was now re-energized—or perhaps more significantly, motivated—by personal convictions.

Lincoln's trip to Peoria in October of 1854 was actually in response to an invitation from the city's Whig Party supporters. The local Whigs wanted Lincoln to challenge Douglas, who was

TOP: Stephen A. Douglas.

RIGHT: Abraham Lincoln.

Photographs courtesy the
Library of Congress.

expected in town for an address touting the Kansas-Nebraska Act,
legislation written by Douglas and recently passed by Congress.
Basically, the Douglas act endorsed the right of voters within states
to determine whether or not it would be legal to own slaves in the
state. The bill effectively reversed the Missouri Compromise of 1820,
ending a ban on slavery in the Louisiana Territories. Lincoln was
vehemently opposed. The invitation letter to Lincoln read in part:
"[We] are exceedingly desirous that (if not too great a tax upon
your time and strength) you will consent to be present and take a
convenient opportunity, after the speech of Judge Douglas, to reply
to it, and give us your own views upon the subject."

Lincoln seized the moment, arriving in Peoria in the wee hours of October 16, the day of the planned speeches. Douglas and his supporters were already in the city and said to be giddy with delight at Lincoln's apparent tardiness. Both men had booked rooms at the same hotel. In Douglas' mind, at least, Lincoln was embarrassingly late. Perhaps he would not be there at all, he thought. Lincoln finally checked in at 2 AM.

Later in the afternoon, Douglas ceremoniously arrived at the speech site in a decorated carriage followed by a marching brass band while Lincoln patiently waited in front of the courthouse at the corner of Adams and Main. "In strange contrast," wrote one observer, "was the quiet, undemonstrative entry of the tall, lank, homely and awkward Lincoln." A platform was constructed on the south corner of the courthouse, partly under the portico. The crowd was packed so close together that entering it from the outside was impossible. The officers and participants, including the 6'4" Lincoln, had to crawl through a first floor window just to reach the stage.

Douglas would speak first, followed by Lincoln, then a final closing remark from Douglas. Most Peorians were on the side of the Democrats, and Douglas' argument, as an adopted Illinoisan and a powerful influence in Washington, was persuasive. Douglas spoke for three hours, delivering an appeal mainly to his supporters in the region. Although no written publication of his speech exists, a reporter for the *Peoria Daily Union* described it this way: "After returning his thanks to the democracy of Peoria for the kind reception extended to him, Judge Douglas proceeded to discuss the principles of the Nebraska bill and to defend himself against the attacks of his opponents."

Douglas cast himself as a martyr standing bravely against the Whigs, who, he claimed, were not united in their opposition to slavery. "Opponents of the Nebraska bill do not like the principle which allows people to settle the slavery question themselves," the *Daily Union* reported him saying. "Is that principle right? Oh. Yes, exclaim some, but say they, you should not disturb the Missouri Compromise."

When Douglas finished, the band played and "six hearty cheers" went up, noted the *Illinois Journal.* Lincoln was next, but first he checked his timepiece. It was near dinnertime, so he decided to wait. He invited the crowd to get something to eat first. "If you hear me now," Lincoln implored, "I wish you to hear me through."

The crowd stirred as Lincoln urged them to return in a couple of hours. Lincoln's words were interpreted in different ways, but his intentions were clear. A combination of several accounts goes like this: "The judge has informed you that he is to have an hour reply to me," Lincoln said of Douglas's rebuttal. "I doubt not, but you have been a little surprised to learn that I have consented to give one of his high reputation and known ability this advantage of me. I can then finish my speech by ten and Douglas can finish his by eleven, which is not an unusually late hour of this season of the year. And, as he has the last speech, if you want to hear him skin me, you had better come."

"What do you say?" Lincoln then asked the crowd directly, perhaps just to see if they were listening. Surprisingly, they were.

A cheer went up, mostly from his supporters, and there were reports of hats being thrown up in the air. Lincoln must have smiled at the reaction. He had given himself time to gather up his thoughts and almost assuredly a large audience for his entire speech. Two hours later, when the crowd banded together again in nearly complete darkness, Lincoln began.

A witness from Peoria named Robert Boal, a doctor, gave this personal account of Lincoln's opening remarks: "Mr. Lincoln slowly arose, and after surveying the large audience, commenced his speech by saying: 'He [Douglas] thought he could appreciate an argument, and at times, believed he could make one, but when one denied the settled and plainest facts of history, you could not argue with him; only the thing you could do would be to stop his mouth with a corn cob.'"

The opening jab was a good one. But whether Lincoln actually said those exact words, especially "the corn cob" remark, is up for debate. When Lincoln returned to Springfield and dictated the Peoria speech, he failed to include it. Instead, Lincoln began more formally, insisting, "my remarks will not be, specifically, an answer to Judge Douglas; yet, as I proceed, the main points he has

Lincoln's Peoria speech on the steps of the old courthouse. Drawing by Charles Overall. SEE PAGE 189 FOR CITATION.

presented will arise, and will receive such respectful attention as I may be able to give them."

Lincoln immediately touched on the hot button issue, the Missouri Compromise, and attacked Douglas for trying to manipulate it. "The Missouri Compromise ought to be restored," he argued. "For the sake of the Union, it ought to be restored. If by any means we omit to do this, what follows?"

Lincoln was at his eloquent best. "The spirit of the mutual concession—that spirit which first gave us the constitution, and which thrice saved the Union—we have strangled and cast from us forever," Lincoln told the crowd. "Rise to the height of a generation of free men, worthy of a free government. The people's will is the ultimate law of the land."

Lincoln's speeches during his presidency and especially the Civil War would be best remembered for their simple but effective words, spoken like a poem in some cases, like the Gettysburg Address. But in Peoria, it was the subject matter that resonated.

"The great mass of mankind," Lincoln stated, "consider slavery a great moral wrong, and their feeling against it is not evanescent, but eternal. It lies at the very foundation of their sense of justice, and cannot be trifled with. It is a great and durable element of popular action, and I think no statesman can safely disregard it."

After Lincoln finished, he yielded the stage back to Douglas. According to witnesses, Douglas' defiant rebuttal "manifested strong symptoms of anger." The senator may have felt defeated or simply at a loss for words. He spoke for less than his allotted hour, it was reported, and seemed feeble in his efforts. His voice was hoarse and worn. Douglas' angry reaction to Lincoln's speech surprised many. Clearly, he had the support of the people that day and an opportunity to intellectually debate Lincoln's words against him. But he chose not to. Instead his disreputable demeanor ended the day.

What occurred after the speech, known as "the Peoria Truce," has also been refuted. According to Lincoln's law partner, William Herndon, Lincoln and Douglas met privately and agreed not to challenge each other with any more debates. Actually it was a request from Douglas, who had bigger aspirations in mind, like the presidency. Lincoln was an outsider in Douglas' opinion and a general pain in the neck. He urged Lincoln to step aside and in return, promised to cancel several speaking engagements in Illinois over the next several days. "I do not wish to crowd you," Lincoln said graciously, and returned to Springfield. Douglas, however, did not keep his promise, according to Herndon.

Regardless of how the night ended in Peoria, four years later, Lincoln and Douglas would meet again as senatorial candidates in a series of debates, seven in all, throughout Illinois. Two years after that, they were opponents for the office of the president.

IN AUGUST of 1860, with Lincoln now a Republican candidate for president, thousands of supporters lined the Springfield streets and held a parade in his honor. The parade route marched right past Lincoln's home, which enabled supporters a chance at least to greet him. Lincoln acknowledged the crowd and was so impressed by its size that he reluctantly agreed to travel by carriage to the state fairgrounds and make a short and reportedly awkward speech before quickly exiting back through the crowd onto a horse and hightailing it back home.

By this point in 1860, just a couple of months prior to the election,

Lincoln presidential poster.
Photograph courtesy
the Library of Congress.

ABRAHAM LINCOLN,
REPUBLICAN CANDIDATE FOR PRESIDENT OF THE UNITED STATES.

opinions about Lincoln as a man and a candidate were beginning to solidify on both sides of the issues. In May of 1860, his popularity had soared during his famed "rail-splitter" speech, in which Lincoln told a feverish crowd how as a young man he split rails and built fences and homes along the Sangamon River. On cue, two old fence rails were brought down the center aisle through the crowd, draped in red, white, and blue streamers and a large banner. Both rails were made by Lincoln and a cousin on land just west of Decatur, the crowd was told. The place "was electrical," wrote one observer, and went wild for Lincoln, who, as the banner proclaimed, became *The Rail Candidate for President 1860* the next day by winning the Republican nomination in a unanimous vote.

To a degree, the split-rail image was also fodder for Lincoln's opponents who sometimes mocked it, but more commonly they were so impressed by its effectiveness that they tried to emulate the use of props and clever names for their own political gain. Supporters of John Bell, the Constitutional Union Party candidate, carried tinkling bells to rallies and called themselves the "bell ringers." Douglas got into the act as well. The Democrats called themselves the "Little Dougs," referring to their candidate's diminutive size and nickname "Little Giant." But neither candidate's ploy worked as well as Lincoln's.

The perception of a rail-splitter was a double-edged sword for Lincoln in another important respect. The hardline Southerners viewed the image, popularized by editorial cartoons, of a man with "broad shoulders, bulging muscles and wielding an axe" as someone who would assail the South.

At the time, there was strong opinion on both sides of the slavery issue, with an obvious geographic split. But there was also a large middle ground of people who believed in compromise. Lincoln's wild card was the Western territories. As America pushed westward and the Republican Party, led by Lincoln, touted the need for a transcontinental railroad, the question was simple: would the newly formed states be slave states or not? Those who were complacent about ending slavery and sympathetic to the plantation owners in the South still saw no advantage to spreading it elsewhere. A Lincoln presidency would support this cause. But what if Lincoln saw fit to end slavery entirely? Where would that lead? The Peoria speech had set the foundation of Lincoln's stance against slavery, but questions remained how he, as president, would proceed.

An editor of a Louisville newspaper wrote Lincoln and asked several questions: "What would you do if elected? Would you interfere? Would it not be wise to say plainly you wouldn't interfere?" Lincoln responded, "Those who have not read, or heeded, what I have already publicly said, would not read, or heed, a repetition of it."

Lincoln's resistance was understandable. An election was at stake, and already a nation was splitting at the seams. The South was slowly pulling away from the Union, and a backlash against the folksy, "uneducated" man from Illinois was growing.

While the early vote tallies narrowly supported Douglas over Lincoln in Illinois, nationally the Electoral College was clearly in favor of the Republicans. On the evening of November 6, 1860, in a building across from the Springfield telegraph office, Lincoln sat down to a dinner prepared by the Republican Ladies Club. When word reached the office that New York had gone with Lincoln, several ladies rushed in. A messenger followed with a telegram that Lincoln had clinched it. "How do you do, Mr. President?" they greeted the seated man.

THE NEXT February, the day before Lincoln would leave the safety of his home to become the 16TH President of the United States, a shiver ran through his good friend, Dr. Melvin, when he read the letters against Lincoln and the threats on his life. Would Lincoln be a target for would-be assassins? Did it start, as the letter implied, before his inaugural speech? Had the scheduled celebratory train ride to Washington been compromised? Lincoln had personally expressed concerns.

Perhaps the very same letters were on Lincoln's mind when he told Herndon, his friend and law partner, not to disturb the rusty hinged sign-board that swung above the stairwell leading to their office. "If I live," Herndon recalls Lincoln telling him, "I'm coming back some time and then we will go right on practicing law as if nothing ever happened." Historians have questioned whether Lincoln actually said, "If I live," claiming Herndon, as he often did, may have embellished the President's words. But the rest of Herndon's farewell story is touching. "[Lincoln] lingered for a moment as if to take a last look at the old quarters, and then passed through the door into the narrow stairwell." With a handshake and "fervent goodbye," Herndon remembers, Lincoln was gone.

The inaugural train left Springfield on February 11, 1861. Before departing, Lincoln waved to his friends and said, "To this place and the kindness of these people I owe everything."

The inaugural whistle-stop tour was set. The train would travel eastward, not north, ignoring the state's largest cities, Chicago and Peoria (it's not as if Lincoln had anything to celebrate there, especially in Peoria, where Douglas defeated Lincoln by a vote of 1,531 to 1,319). Instead, the route and schedule were a well-calculated effort to maximize time, efficiency and safety. The train would stop at only two cities in Illinois and then continue through Indiana, Ohio, Pennsylvania and New York before heading to the capital. Along the way, there would be big crowds.

In tiny Tolono, just south of Champaign, Lincoln would say farewell to his beloved Illinois. From the back of the train, he delivered a passionate 20-minute speech focusing on slavery and the preservation of the Union. A large crowd had gathered in Tolono, larger than the president-elect and his handlers had anticipated, so Lincoln reportedly delivered the speech he had planned for Danville, the last stop in his home state.

A light rain was falling, and Lincoln's tone was somber. "A sob went through the listening crowd as the broken voice asked their prayers," a local scribe wrote. "There they stood, these townsmen of Abraham Lincoln, with bared heads, the raindrops mingling with tears."

Lincoln told them, "I am leaving you on an errand of national importance, attended, as you are aware, with considerable difficulties."

In the crowd, a young girl yelled out that she could not see the president-elect, so a baggage man lifted her up.

Lincoln continued, "Let us believe, as some poet has expressed it, 'Behind the cloud the sun is still shining.' I bid you an affectionate farewell."

Lincoln turned and walked back to his coach car. In the distance, a cannon fired and the hundreds in attendance "waved handkerchiefs" as the train moved on.

"The bell on the funny-looking engine clanged," a reporter wrote, "a warning of the beginning of a Great Adventure."

After the two stops in Illinois, Lincoln's inaugural train made nearly 100 more stops en route to Washington. Most were brief and occurred mainly at towns in Ohio, Pennsylvania and New York. Since Lincoln didn't travel much during the campaign, this was a chance for the rest of the country to meet and greet the man. Lincoln's message didn't change much from his speech in Illinois, but unlike the tears and solemn goodbyes that Lincoln delivered to his home state, the crowds that greeted him the rest of the way were jovial, and the president-elect seemed energized by their good spirits.

In the annals of history, the train trip to Washington is mostly remembered for Lincoln's encounter with a sweet little girl and an unusual request. A few weeks before the election, 11-year-old Grace Bedell sent a letter to Lincoln urging him to grow a beard. "You would look a great deal better," she wrote, "for your face is so thin." Lincoln was amused, but not convinced. "Do you not think people would call it a silly affection if I were to begin it now?" he responded in kind. When the two met during a brief stop in Bedell's hometown of Westfield, New York, Lincoln had apparently changed his mind. He was sporting an early growth on his chin. Before departing, the newly elected president sat down with the little girl and said, "Look at my whiskers, I have been growing them for you."

Lincoln's new beard may have also been a natural concealment. Several days later came "The Baltimore Plot." Facing plausible threats that a band of men would hijack the train and kill him, Lincoln, at the urging of the Pinkerton Detective Agency, changed rail cars and tracks in the middle of the night and passed through Baltimore several hours ahead of schedule and without much notice. The move did not sit well with the press. Lincoln was falsely accused of abandoning his wife and family (Mary and the boys were not on the train). He also did not don a disguise, as widely reported. Later, Lincoln would regret the decision, calling it, effectively, an unpropitious start to his presidency.

DESPITE THE threats on his life, Lincoln would, of course, make it to Washington and begin his first term. The first inaugural address in March 1861 was without incident. Lincoln faced a nation divided over the very same issue he initiated in Peoria some seven years before. "One section of our country believes slavery is *right* and ought to be extended," he said on the East Portico of the Capitol, "while the other believes it is *wrong* and ought not to be extended. This is the only substantial dispute." The next month, on April 12, Confederate troops fired on Fort Sumter. The Civil War was under way.

Four years later, on March 4, 1865, Lincoln stood on the Capitol steps again and delivered his second inaugural address. The nation had changed considerably. The South was reeling, thousands of slaves were already free, and General Lee's surrender was imminent. Amongst the crowd gathered in Washington to hear the President speak was a short man with dark, wavy hair and a distinguished mustache. Some recognized him as an actor in town. His name was John Wilkes Booth. A month later, on April 14, Lincoln was dead.

Seven days after he was shot, Lincoln would begin his journey back to Springfield. Like the inaugural trip, a train carrying the President's body would make numerous stops in New York, Penn-

Lincoln's funeral train.
Photograph courtesy the
Library of Congress

sylvania and Ohio, stopping in larger cities for long, protracted ceremonies. When the train reached Illinois, however, the route was
changed to accommodate demands by officials in the state's largest city that Lincoln's cortege pass through its gates. A large arch
was built in Lake Park as the train slowly chugged into Chicago.
A procession, by foot and horseback, then proceeded along several
downtown streets to the Courthouse Square on Clark Street. More
than 120,000 people marched that day.

From Chicago, the train traveled south, passing through cities
like Joliet, Pontiac, Bloomington and Lincoln (named in 1854 for
Lincoln, the lawyer, who helped settle land claims for the new city).
Large crowds gathered in the middle of the night to watch mourn-
fully as the train went by. Some reached out for the slow-moving
vessel, some stood in silence, and others waved handkerchiefs in
respect.

Illinois' second-largest city was again off the list of stops. Although
Peoria was in the center of the state and a hub for more than a dozen
rail lines, the funeral train's route would not deviate from a mostly
straight line southwest from Chicago to Springfield. More than 30
cities, towns and villages in Illinois were honored and moved by the
site of the railroad car carrying the President's body as it soberly
passed in the darkness, but Peoria was not one of them.

Tolono was not on the route either. The small community that
would forever carry the banner of hosting one of Lincoln's final

stops in his home state would not be included in his trip back. Today in Tolono, there is a marker commemorating the site and date of Lincoln's farewell address: February 11, 1861. "It was a dreary, dank, drizzly day..." the sign reads.

That was the day Lincoln left Illinois for the last time.

SEVERAL YEARS after Lincoln was buried, the literary bureau that the president-elect handed Mrs. Grimsley before leaving Springfield was examined and vetted. "Dispose of them as deemed proper," Lincoln had implored, suggesting he might not return. By "dispose," Lincoln meant to distribute and share them. He was asking that they be preserved. His friends understood his wishes.

The bureau was opened.

It contained three of his lectures, each transcribed by Lincoln.

Unlike the *Peoria Speech,* which was published almost immediately after it was set to paper, Lincoln had written the words to the three lectures without anyone's notice or demand. All three were titled *Discoveries and Inventions* and contained thoughts and ideas for planning and constructing a future that better utilized "iron tools" and wood for building and manufacturing, and natural resources like water and wind to move people and products more efficiently. "All creation is a mine," Lincoln wrote, beginning one of the lectures, "and every man is a miner."

We can now assert that Lincoln gave the lectures in 1860, the year before he became president and several months before the "rail-splitter" speech thrust him into the political spotlight. These talks about how to better fortify a nation through ingenuity and process went unnoticed for years. Without Lincoln's insistence, however, they may have been lost forever. Lincoln, of course, wanted them remembered. "I will claim them again," Lincoln inferred, if and when he made it back to Springfield.

In 1909, the centennial of Lincoln's birth and nearly a half-century after his death, they were published for the first time.

BURY THE HATCHET

By the time Prohibition was enacted on January 17, 1920, most Americans were ready. Thanks to a fortified grass-roots effort, especially in the religious South, many states had already gone dry. The states with larger cities, industries and urban landscapes like Illinois were not among them. So when the bell finally sounded that January night calling for hardcore guzzlers and casual tipplers alike to call it quits, they shakily raised their glasses one last time, made an emotional toast to days gone by, and did what they did best—kept on drinking. Prohibition wasn't an easy sell. In Peoria, where whiskey was made—lots of it—the banning of hard liquor meant good men would be out of work and massive distilleries along the Illinois River's banks would cease production. Barrels upon barrels of whiskey would be stored away, or worse, destroyed. Yet people still wanted to drink. And the idea of a nationwide ban on alcohol certainly didn't take anyone by surprise. In fact, it had been boiling over for decades thanks to organizations and individuals who led protests and preached the virtues of a country rid of its evil sins, like drinking. Many colorful characters added to its lore, including Wayne B. Wheeler, the de facto leader of the Anti-Saloon League, whose strong-arm tactics like targeting congressmen who resisted his demands, known as the "wets," would make even today's most hardened political operatives blush. Then there was Carrie Nation. The temperance movement and suffrage leader from Kansas went right to the source, the saloons and saloon owners, calling for justice, causing destruction, and leaving a mess of broken mirrors and bottles in her wake. She became an instant celebrity and everyone—no matter whose side you were on—wanted to know what she would do next. In the midst of all this scrutiny, one day, she came to Peoria. Her mission was clear, but her visit was anything but predictable. There were other things on her mind that day, and she was hell-bent on initiating them. And as the old saying goes, when you go looking for trouble...

IN 1873 Paris, amongst the art elite who gathered for the illustrious annual event known as the Salon, a large painting was unveiled that both shocked and thrilled those who were privileged to view it. The man responsible for the massive painting—nearly 9 feet tall and 6 feet wide—was William Bouguereau, a rather quiet and elusive figure who was besieged with words of praise and condemnation. "A rather risky work of charm and delicacy," enthused one critic, while another more tersely remarked that the work was "cold in essence, empty and leaving but a faint impression." But despite the somewhat contemptible reception, most art connoisseurs were convinced Bouguereau had created something quite noteworthy, just not life-changing.

Bouguereau appropriately named his painting *Nymphs and Satyr* as it portrays a scene by a pond where four naked women, the nymphs, are leading a reluctant half-man-half-goat, the Satyr of Greek mythology, to a bath. Inspired by a quote from a first-century poem, Bouguereau had the influential passage imprinted next to the painting's display so others would understand his inspiration. It read: "Conscious of his shaggy hide and from childhood untaught to swim, he dares not trust himself to deep waters." The meaning aside, what was most striking about the painting were the figures themselves, especially the naked nymphs, full-figured and playfully limber with several backsides and breasts exposed. Their intentions, at least to most onlookers, had nothing to do with getting the Satyr clean. "Bouguereau's plump-bottomed girls," one critic expertly declaimed, "are vainly trying to get their shaggy, Pan-piping friend to romp with them."

Bouguereau was considered a traditional artist at a time when Impressionist painters like Renoir and Monet were gaining popularity and increasing fame. So he may have felt detached from a growing movement. But Bouguereau loved the simplicity and beauty of the human figure and was quite proud of his work—haute art connoisseurs be damned. A New York art collector named John Wolfe, familiar with Bouguereau paintings, saw its value as a conversation piece. "It will be a principal attraction of future exhibitions," he said. Wolfe bought the painting and displayed it in his New York home gallery, where art lovers both marveled and tittered

William Bouguereau, *Nymphs and Satyr* c. 1873. Photograph courtesy Wiki-Art.org.

at its striking but salacious imagery. Resting upon Wolfe's gallery walls, it immediately caught the attention of a local hotel owner.

Enter Edward S. Stokes, just "Ned" to his closet friends. Stokes was a New York Tammany Hall conformist, all business and even more pleasure at a time when the city was being run by those who favored breaking the law, not following it. Stokes had just served time for killing a business partner over a money dispute, although the trouble started—and escalated—when the business partner, a man named Jim Fisk, introduced Stokes to his girlfriend, actress Josie Mansfield, with whom Stokes had fallen instantly and madly in love and whose adorations and affections were mutually shared.

Now this Fisk character was no birthday cake either. Wealthy and powerful, he flaunted his riches, sometimes quite diligently to charities, but mostly upon himself. He perfumed his hair, waxed his mustache, and spiffed up in the finest duds: flashy velvet coats and perfectly pressed silk shirts accentuated by impressive diamond studs and cufflinks. His reputation preceded him. "An entertainer, a clown, a scoundrel and a fop," one writer described Fisk at the time, who earned the nickname "Gentleman Jim" for his generosity and loyalty to his friends. Growing up in stolid Vermont and cutting his teeth in door-to-door sales, Fisk was dubbed "Santa Claus" by the neighborhood children because he often showed up at homes with "gifts"—mostly overpriced trinkets and tools—he peddled to struggling farm families. Later, when he was dealing with other people's money, mainly stocks, Fisk would announce his arrival with a puff of smoke from a fancy cigar, then press the stub firmly between his fingers and punctuate his words with fist jabs, sending smoke and ash in the faces of his adversaries.

In New York City, Fisk was a larger-than-life figure both in personality and size who loved the grandeur of the theater, pretty women, and the art of the deal, usually a corrupt one, which put cash in his pockets and power in his hands. A self-taught con man, Fisk hit pay dirt during the Civil War by smuggling cotton from Southern plantations to Northern mills.

Fisk cavorted with men of similar tastes and ambitions, mostly financers and Wall Street types, like railroad tycoon and fellow shyster Jay Gould. On a September day in 1869, known as "Black Friday," Gould and Fisk conspired to take over the gold market, buying in large amounts and driving the prices up, until President Grant—fooled once by the impressionable hucksters—intervened. As brokers, they could have made a fortune risking other people's money, and they came out of the scandal mostly unscathed. Others weren't so lucky.

As business partners, Ned Stokes and Jim Fisk got along for a time. Stokes inherited an oil business, and Fisk saw a good opportunity to cash in. When Stokes and Mansfield began an affair, however, all bets were off. In a petty but bitter war of words and recriminations, Stokes accused Fisk of fraud and Fisk accused Stokes of

LEFT TO RIGHT: Josie Mansfield, Jim Fisk and Edward Stokes. Photographs from author's personal collection.

embezzlement. Mansfield was stuck in the middle, but clearly sided with her new lover. Fisk, however, was filthy rich, and Mansfield sought to exploit it. She sued Fisk, claiming he owed her money in escrow, then threatened to release a "trunk load" of letters that he wrote to her, which admitted past affairs and, even worse, suspect business dealings. Fisk fumed and retaliated.

In the end, Fisk had more cash and wielded more legal might. A blackmail charge he threw against Mansfield and the suspected schemer, Ned Stokes, was solid. The grand jury agreed, and Stokes was indicted.

When Stokes found out about the indictment, he snapped. On

January 6, 1872, after confronting Fisk on a hotel staircase, Stokes pulled out a pistol and, without saying a word, fired two rounds into his nemesis' belly. Stokes made a feeble attempt to escape but, upon being chased, slipped on the hotel's marble flooring just before reaching the front door. Fisk hung on long enough to identify his killer. "Have you any hopes of recovering?" they asked him. "I hope so," Fisk replied. He died the next day.

In typical New York fashion, once Stokes returned from serving four years in Sing-Sing prison, he was welcomed back with open arms by his Tammany Hall cronies. Stokes partnered with a loyal friend who owned the Hoffman House, a trendy hotel in New York. They opened a bar in the hotel and needed something impressive to put on the walls. Stokes took up the challenge. While browsing the art galleries of New York, specifically the home of international art buyer John Wolfe, he discovered the painting *Nymphs and Satyr* and bought it on the spot.

Stokes had finally done something right. He proudly displayed the painting across from the square-shaped mahogany bar at the Hoffman House, and it became an overnight sensation. Soon everyone was talking about it. Even curious women would glance at it quite brazenly through the barroom's open doors. In general, American critics were kind, invoking its sense of place rather than implicating moral judgments: "The exhibition of the big Bouguereau in an up-town barroom has paid off because the peculiar character of the subject makes it popular with frequenters of the place," was one writer's rather wry opinion, adding, "Altogether, it may be said, that it is happy in its surroundings."

Indeed it was. Visitors came to the bar just to see the large painting, its glossy canvas vibrantly displayed underneath a red canopy, lit by a crystal chandelier and reflected in a large mirror—a convenient location where patrons, mostly men, could sit with their backs turned and still enjoy its many assets. The image became so aligned with the bar itself, Stokes had it meticulously reproduced on the inside of his hotel's cigar boxes, matchbook covers, urns, and bathroom tiles. The painting gained even more popularity when it was caricatured in the local papers. The drawing depicts the work hanging in an art gallery as a man named "Weary Walker" stares longingly at the beautiful naked nymphs by the running water. "I've travelled the world over and tramped every spot on the map," he muses, "but I be dammed [sic] if I can't locate that brook."

Stokes entertained many distinguished guests at the hotel, including a future president, Warren G. Harding, who was a big supporter of alcohol rights. Another frequent visitor was P.T. Barnum. Legend has it that when Barnum was in the bar, typical of his reputation as a showman and prankster, the "Bouguereau's girls"– the nymphs in the famous painting–would come to life. With this kind of notoriety, and much to Stokes' delight, *Nymphs and Satyr*, it can be argued, became the most famous painting in New York.

This brings us to Peter Weast of Peoria. The showy saloon and vaudeville theater owner was convinced that Bouguereau's work belonged in one of his establishments, too. He found a copy in Berlin, Germany, while on a business trip and bought it for $4,000. The painting, of course, was not Bouguereau's original *Nymphs and Satyr*–it was already famous in New York–but a glorified reproduction right down to its massive size. Weast brought it home to Peoria, put it on the wall of one of his saloons, and waited for a reaction. The cyclone that eventually blew through his doors and nearly knocked it over came from Kansas.

Her name was Carrie Nation.

IT WAS very early on February 25, 1901, when a passenger train from the west chugged into Peoria's Union Station. In the faint light of the street lamps now shrouded even further by the drifting cloud of steam, several carriages lined up waiting to transport weary passengers. One lady in particular was anticipating a ride. Dressed in a long, black drapery dress, shawl, veil, and white ribbon tie, she presented the appearance of "a well favored matron," the papers reported, "familiarized by the familiar pictures now in circulation all over the country." She slipped into a carriage, "quiet as a mouse," and was escorted to the Cosmopolitan Hotel on South Monroe Street, just a few blocks away.

Later that morning at the offices of the *Peoria Journal* newsroom, a telegraph bell sounded, signifying that a new message had arrived. Outside, a young boy was anxiously waiting. When the bell went off, he jumped with excitement and ran to the newspaper office door. Poking his head inside, the boy turned to the telegraph operator and asked, "Is Carrie in?" The boy's inquisitiveness gave the usually stoic newspapermen pause. The editor had asked the staff to ratchet up the excitement of the day's upcoming activities, and earlier editions had done just that. But this was more than they had anticipated. The *Journal* playfully reported that "A wee, weasel-face mite with ragged and unkempt hair and a neglected nose slid into the sanctum [newsroom]." The "weasel-faced mite," of course, wanted to know if the "hatchet-wielding grandma" from Kansas had arrived in town as promised. He wasn't alone. Soon, more people gathered outside the newspaper building waiting to hear the news.

The editorial office has been reduced to a "prolonged interrogation point," the paper recounted in its early editions. "Everybody wants to know. Don't you know?" they incredulously asked their readers. Soon, everyone did know. In the middle of the night, she had arrived. Carrie Nation, the most prolific anti-drink crusader in the country, was in Peoria, Illinois.

Just a day before coming to Peoria, Nation was in a Topeka, Kansas, jail cell whistling hymns, reading from the Bible, and knitting. A judge had refused to release her until she signed a pledge not to do the very thing that put her behind bars in the first place—marching into a saloon, hatchet in hand, and trashing the joint. Her latest victim was one of the largest bars in Topeka, the Senate Saloon, so named because its clientele included many top government officials from the state capital. Nation and her angry mob walked in, proclaimed the establishment "the work of the devil," and proceeded to hack away until every bottle, mirror, door, and window was in pieces on the floor. The "smashers," as the reporters dubbed them, were arrested and sent to jail. The county and state attorneys decided against police court since Nation and her followers meant no harm to any person. But they demanded a hearing in circuit court. The charge was disturbing the peace.

Nation later described the attack: "I smashed the mirror, and all the bottles under it; picked up the cash register, threw it down; then broke the faucets of the refrigerator, opened the door and cut the rubber tubes that conducted the beer...I opened the bungs of the beer kegs, and opened the faucets of the barrels, and then the beer flew in every direction and I was completely saturated."

Nation likely didn't mind being in jail. She was making a point. But being incarcerated also meant that she and her mighty hatchet could not inflict any more damage, a temporary respite for which Kansas saloon owners were surely thankful.

Nation pledged to appeal the case, claiming she was nearly poisoned by nicotine (one of the saloon patrons was smoking, she argued), but the judge refused. Nation would be freed on bail only if she signed an agreement not to smash any more liquor establishments. It was her turn to refuse. So in jail she stayed. Nation made the best of it. She cheerfully talked to reporters, prayed, started a newspaper called *The Smasher's Mail,* and caught up on her knitting. "I want you to stop your fooling and let me out of here," she eventually wrote the judge. "Let me out that I may go about my business of saving such poor devils as you." But the judge's ruling was firm. Then an enticing offer came from a newspaperman in Illinois. W.A. Brubaker, publisher of the *Journal* and a prohibition supporter, offered Nation $150 to come to Peoria, lecture, and edit the newspaper for a day. Nation was intrigued. After all, Peoria was the world's largest whiskey maker by volume. She accepted but needed help.

She allowed supporters to post bond on her behalf. But she still refused to sign the pledge. Fearing an angry backlash, the judge let Nation go on a personal promise that she would return to jail once her business in Peoria was completed. "For I have more knitting to attend," she told reporters. Then the 54-year-old Carrie Amelia Nation, who also spelled her first name Carry and whose middle initial gave the sensationalist press an ironic catchphrase—"Carry A. Nation"—boarded a Santa Fe train bound for Illinois. She immediately sent a telegram to Peoria: "I'm on my way."

CARRIE NATION was "six feet tall, with the biceps of a stevedore, the face of a prison warden and the persistence of a toothache," as one writer rather colorfully described her. He could have added that she weighed 180 pounds or more and was fearless about

Carrie A. Nation. Photograph courtesy the Library of Congress.

physical confrontations, particularly with drunk men. She was as tough as a hammer.

Nation was born in November 1846 on a farm in rural Kentucky. Her parents were faithful churchgoers, but not as strict as the extremist Shakers who camped nearby and may have had an indirect influence on young Carrie. Nation's father, George Moore, was no Shaker—his family made good money buying land—but he was a "strict moralist" who demanded that all his children, even the girls, do manual labor on the farm. When Carrie became a teenager, however, he bought her a spinning wheel and ordered her to make him some pants.

Carrie's mother was different. Distant and cold at times, especially to her children, the pathos of Mary Moore's personality might be easily explained by the tragic fate of her first family. Losing her husband and two sons in quick succession, a despondent Mary moved to her parents' farm and subsequently met George. He was a widower with two children in tow. Carrie was their first child together, followed by several more.

While her mother attended to the babies—averaging "one every eighteen months"—Carrie lived in the slave quarters with an elderly black woman named Eliza. There she played with "white and black children" and watched as the slaves "sang sweet dirges," shouting and shaking their bodies in religious rapture. At times, Carrie would join in. At night in Eliza's cabin, Carrie would listen to ghost stories about evil slave masters in "clanking chains" doomed to wander graveyards at night, then sent back to hell at the cock's crow to be roasted on gridirons and poked by the devil's pitchfork. Later, in her autobiography, Carrie wrote that her father was "kind to the slaves."

Carrie was fairly close to her father, although they argued and disagreed constantly. George was a domineering man, and Carrie was fiercely independent. Still, as a child she adored him, even filing her teeth down so she could match the shape of his rotting nubs, worn away by an enduring love affair with the corn pipe.

Although it can be debated where Carrie turned on the evils of alcohol, her first marriage to husband Charles can be considered high on the list. After a lengthy engagement, Charles Gloyd and Carrie married in 1867. Both were in their twenties and had known each other a long time, but they had spent little time together— their relationship was conducted mainly through the mail. It took Carrie's parents some time to warm up to Charles, a doctor, but Carrie was drawn to the possibility of a life away from the farm and, even more tantalizing, an education.

Five days after the wedding, things turned sour. Charles returned home stinking drunk and paid little attention to Carrie. He passed out cold on the bed and proceeded to snore his inebriation away. The next night it happened again. A disappointed Carrie sobbed uncontrollably each time.

One night Charles stayed out late, and Carrie's curiosity over-came her. She made her way down to the newly established Mason's lodge and banged on the door. Peering inside, the stench of alcohol assailed her nose, and the sound of clinking tankards and laugh-ter filled her ears. Instead of drinking alone in shame, which she had suspected, Charles had a socially acceptable place to get drunk. "Women aren't allowed," she was told as the door slammed in her face. Carrie was appalled.

Worse, she was also pregnant. Carrie moved back home to her parents and had a baby daughter named Charlien. Carrie did not hate Charles; she only resented his behavior. Her strict parents, however, forbade her to go back. A year later, Charles was dead.

In 1874, Carrie remarried, this time to David Nation, a levelhead-ed widower farmer with five children from a previous marriage. He relocated his new wife, her baby, and the rest of the children to Missouri, Texas, and eventually Kansas. The marriage worked but was far from perfect. David was a good husband but always busy on the farm. He had little time to spend with the family. Car-rie was saddled with the burden of raising her own daughter plus five stepchildren. When they moved to Kansas in 1889, Carrie was secretly making a pact with God. A baptism and revival at a Meth-odist conference in Texas had changed her life, both spiritually and socially. She vowed to live her life for and by God's principles, naysayers be damned.

By the time she reached Peoria, Nation was already a quasi-celebrity. Now in concert with effort to gain women's suffrage, the organized stance against "immoral behaviors" mostly favored by men, like drinking, smoking, and lewd public displays of entertain-ment such as burlesque shows, attracted the ire of not only women who were fighting for equal representation but religious zealots as well. Because of its widespread acceptance and availability, alcohol was at the top of the target list. In Kansas, large groups of women who once crossed the street to avoid saloons were now walking straight through the front doors, led by Nation, hatchets in hand, ready to do battle.

Nation had a clear vengeance against the "evils" like alcohol, but widespread support of both the suffrage and temperance movement, especially by women who weren't smashing saloons, was motivated by economic concerns too, like how to maintain a family and feed the children in a home supported by men who drank away the food and living expenses every day.

Nation would talk about "cleaning house" and constantly stress the need for a more responsible society. "I am not afraid of men," she said. "I like 'em. I want to help." But as long as whiskey was available, men were devils. She tried to sooth their beastly ways. "Men, take care of your homes," she urged. "Love is the greatest thing in the world and if there is anything which whiskey murders, it is love." Nation's stern attitude and tactics, like a mother reprimanding a spoiled child, became the face of the temperance movement. Her stint in jail is what made national headlines. Now most of the country knew who she was and what she was up to. A newspaperman in Peoria seized the moment.

IN PEORIA, Brubaker's plan was already making waves. "Nation's [newspaper] edition is in keen demand," the *Journal* professed. "Chicago telegraphed orders of 9,500 and 22,000 extras are needed to supply the demand in and around the city."

Nation's visit to Peoria had two purposes. She would edit the *Journal,* and she would lecture, the paper reported: "In this way the people here and hereabouts will reach a fair understanding of what the Kansas crusade means and is liable to lead out to."

There was one stipulation, however. Nation's imitable sword of justice, the revered and equally reviled hatchet, was not welcome.

"The hatchet has accomplished more in Kansas than men's voices," Nation would proudly proclaim, espousing her exploits back home. But this day would be different. "She could not smash," the papers reported, "she had promised she would not."

When Nation finally arrived in Peoria late Monday night, she went to a downtown hotel for rest. The train ride from Kansas had already been eventful. Several reports had Nation arising from her coach seat and sniffing the air like a dog sensing food. Then she stormed into the smoking cars and snatched cigars from the mouths of unsuspecting men and liquor from their hands. One man was said to have approached Carrie. He danced a poor excuse for a jig, it was reported, and sang a bouncy tune:

"Hurray, Samantha. Mrs. Nation is in town! So get on your bonnet and your Sunday evening gown; Oh, I am so blamed excited, I am hopping up and down! Hurrah! Hurrah! Samantha. Carrie Nation is in town."

At the hotel, Nation's brief rest was interrupted by her own conscience. "I had not one line for the paper," she recalled in her autobiography, "so I got up at 4 AM and wrote continuously that day." After furiously putting her thoughts down on paper and turning in the copy, Nation was let loose on the city. In a schedule carefully orchestrated by Brubaker, she set out on foot.

The first stop was the Great Western distillery. Nation was greeted kindly by the manager, Mr. Casey, who told her the majority of whiskey made at the plant "does not go down men's throats," as she had suggested. In fact, added Casey, the workers are not permitted to drink the product (while working). Unconvinced, Nation sarcastically remarked, "What would you think of a dry goods concern that would not allow its employees to use what it makes?"

Nation told the man he should "do what's right" and destroy "the whole shop." Casey must have chewed his lip at that notion. He suggested a tour, "to show how whiskey is made," and invited his guest.

Nation walked among the floor maltings, mash tuns, fermenting vessels, copper pots, kilns, and casks. In the air was an overbearing scent of corn, wheat, and molasses, boiling and cooling. It was said that the odor could carry "three miles away." It was an aroma that Peorians knew well. "Everything about the plant was explained to her in detail," the papers reported. But Nation was pleased with only one aspect of the operation, the livestock, to which she remarked directly, "I'm glad you animals are not fed upon that which intoxicates. You are treated better than the children of men."

When asked what she thought of the distillery in general, "It is hell," was her curt response. With that, the tour was over, and Mr. Casey gladly offered to give her a ride back downtown in his private carriage.

The next stop was Rouse's Opera Hall, where Brubaker had arranged a speaking engagement to members of the Methodist

Church. About 400 people packed the room. Nation was anxious to speak.

In the dressing room, as Nation, Brubaker and Dr. Buckley, the Methodist pastor, waited for the crowd to be seated, a tense standoff occurred that would set the tone for the rest of the evening. Brubaker and Buckley were going to give a short talk and prayer before the ceremonies began. Brubaker insisted Nation wait until they finish their remarks before entering the hall stage. Her appearance, he said, "would be too much of a demonstration for Buckley to offer prayer." Nation protested.

Brubaker pleaded, "You must let me have my way in this."

"But, I won't," Nation said sternly.

"Really Mrs. Nation, can't you see..." Brubaker tried to explain before being cut off.

"No, sir. I can't see anything," Nation retorted. "I am going out to that platform right this very minute and you are coming after me. Come along, I tell you." She nudged her way between the two men and marched out of the room. The brief misunderstanding, in Nation's opinion, was over. She won.

"Brubaker and Pastor Buckley did as the prophetess predicted," the papers reported.

After Buckley's blessing, which was "at some length," Nation sprang up and shouted for someone to get the Bible she had left in the dressing room. A reporter obliged. Then she began.

"I'm going to kill the hen that lays the eggs," Nation preached to a supportive audience, referring to the saloons. "And the only men who will be appreciative of me are the ones whose saloons I am now smashing." She urged the congregation to sing hymns, and together they recited Psalm 23: "...*Even though I walk through the darkest valley, I will fear no evil, for you are with me; your rod and your staff, they comfort me.*"

After the speech, Brubaker insisted Nation call it a night. But the fiery activist had other plans. She was interested in visiting a particular bar. The bar owner had a certain painting on the wall, she was told. "Show me how to find this Mr. Weast," Nation demanded.

Brubaker, perhaps surprised by her demand, sternly objected.

"I defy you to stop me," she said, taking the arms of two reporters who escorted her to the front door. Before she stepped out, an attorney blocked her path. "I wouldn't go to see Mr. Weast if I were you," he warned. But it was too late.

"You child of the devil," Nation shrieked, "I know my business. I know what I'm doing." At that point, the "Kansas Cyclone," as the papers called her, stormed out.

With determination, Nation marched to the Golden Palace Saloon, took off her veil and shawl, and went in the side entrance. "This place is the place of the devil," she shouted, and spotted a man standing at the counter drinking a beer. "Oh, my, my boy," she prodded, "my boy, throw that away. Please do." She approached the man, but he ran off through the crowd. She looked around and spotted the picture in question, the massive, gold-framed *Nymphs and Satyr.*

"I'll smash it if you don't," Nation told Weast, who was waiting for her.

Just then, a police detective named Kerr, who was trailing Nation at the request of Brubaker, stepped in. "When will you smash it?" he demanded, defying Nation to make the first move. "When will you smash it? I want to know when you are going to smash it."

"I will smash it tomorrow if you don't," she replied. She then gave the detective a tongue-lashing. "Look here you, officer. Mr. Weast is ashamed at this picture. He knows it is the form of his mother; his heart cries out in shame. But you, Mr. Officer, you stand here trying to justify this thing."

She reprimanded the detective for being a "perjurer" and "scoundrel" before ending the conversation like a mother tempering an angry child. "You are a nice officer," she concluded. "Yes, and a servant of the people, oh, what a nice servant." Then she turned her attention back to Weast.

Peter Weast was no pushover. Flashy and jovial, with a portly middle and a thick mustache that covered his entire upper lip, Weast wore a large diamond stud in his tautly pressed shirts and always greeted patrons with a tip of his fine silk hat. His business was alcohol, but he was no indulger. "Whiskey is a good thing to make, to buy and to sell," he once said, adding somewhat sarcastically, "but a bad thing to drink."

RIGHT: Peter Weast.

FAR RIGHT: Ad in *Peoria Journal* the day of Carrie Nation's visit.

Courtesy the Local History and Genealogy Collection, Peoria Public Library, Peoria, IL.

SPECIAL SALE ON

HATCHETS
TO-DAY

Every Hatchet, Broadaxe or Axe in our store will
be sold today at a discount of 20 per cent. Don't miss
this opportunity of getting the best at reduced prices.

H. SANDMEYER & CO.
216 S. Adams Street

In town, Weast had a reputation as a businessman who took no bull. During a visit overseas, Weast was so unimpressed with Europeans that he shortened his trip and hurried back home. "I would not trade my back porch of Peoria for all of Europe," he told the local papers. Always the gracious host, however, when the irrepressible Carrie Nation came barging through his saloon doors, Weast was ready to show her a good time.

Weast invited Nation to the back of the bar, the vaudeville stage, to witness a performance. She took a seat and seemed pleased by the orchestra music—but that's all. Not letting a good opportunity pass, she went up to the stage to speak. Brubaker again objected, and Nation was told that she was under contract only to speak at Rouse's Hall. If she spoke anywhere else, she would not be paid. "Then I'll walk home," she shot back defiantly.

"You are a class of people who think that here you can find comfort and pleasure, but you are deceived," she told the audience. "I would be the happiest woman in the world if I could just smash Mr. Weast's saloon tonight. He has told me that he will take down the picture, and I believe he will do it." The crowd was pleasant but bemused. Perhaps even a snicker or two filled the small theater.

With that, the night was over. Carrie Nation had had her say; exhausted, she retreated back to the hotel. By morning, a train would be waiting to take her back to Kansas.

The next day, Nation returned to Topeka and her jail cell as promised. But the visit to Peoria was clearly the attention-grabber Brubaker had expected. Nation was soon in high demand as a curiosity and performer. After her release, Nation embarked on a nationwide campaign, visiting cities and wielding her hatchet, but mostly as a speaker and not a smasher. "People either adored or despised her," wrote Fran Grace in *Carry A. Nation: Retelling the Life,* "but they rarely ignored her." Edward Hardy, a bar owner in Austin, Texas, was the first to request her services. Reading about her antics at Weast's bar in the papers, Hardy immediately sent a telegram to Nation inviting her to speak in front of the Texas legislature and to visit his establishment, the Big Four Saloon. Without hesitation, Nation relayed a message back: "If you will allow me to smash your murder shop," she wrote, "I will be your guest. But under no other circumstance."

The *Nymphs and Satyr* painting never came down as Nation claims Weast had promised, although he may have covered it for a time. Instead, the bar owner sent a $50 check to Nation's organization, the Home Defenders, as a peace offering.

The much-ballyhooed edition of the day's paper was also a bust for Nation. Although she had submitted many articles, the agitated Brubaker decided not to run them. Instead, he relegated Nation's coverage to the eighth page and in between included a reporter's take on the day's events and several viewpoints from local organizations and leaders. One story asked the question, "What is a nuisance?" The answer, by that point, was obvious.

Nation was not pleased. "Jesus said, 'beware of wolves in sheep's clothing,'" she wrote in her memoirs, referring to Brubaker's rejection. She later admitted that her articles were critical of the newspaper and its liquor ads. But she never apologized. Some of the rejected articles were reprinted in her autobiography. Carrie's own words, as one writer described them, "were about as lucid as a swamp." There wasn't a sentence or word she would change:

Whiskey or tobacco never introduce their products by reason or arguments, they never appeal to thought, but suggestion or temptation; every one of their signs has false basis. For instance, 'Old Crow Whisky.' This is slandering the crow. 'Bull Durham Tobacco.' There's not a dog or bull that uses tobacco.... I have

seen a life-size picture of Abraham Lincoln advertising a cigar,
when Lincoln was a teetotaler from cigars or any intoxicating
drink. He promised his mother he would never use them and
kept his promise to his death. This is slandering the dead.

When Nation was released from the Topeka jail, the ranks of her
followers were already diminishing. Most of the women who proudly marched into the Senate Saloon with her, hatchets in hand, could
not sustain the movement without their de facto leader. The rioting
in the streets of Topeka that followed Nation's arrest were mostly protests against her incarceration and demands for her release,
nothing more. Many of her supporters just didn't have Carrie's
venomous urgency to continue the cause. They went back to their
daily lives of household chores and family tending, while Nation
continued.

This did not, however, slow the temperance movement in general.
Nationwide, women's groups still touted the need for more strin-
gent alcohol laws, and groups like the Anti-Saloon League—made
up mostly of men—were a well-organized force, backed by Protes-
tant churches, which spread its brand of moral standards and judgments through intimidation and persuasion rather than destruction. Nation's antics were bush-league, in their opinion. "I don't
believe in fanatics," an ASL member once said about movements
like Nation's. "They do not accomplish what common sense does."

In Peoria, Nation's daylong visit was mostly remembered for her
surprise trip to Weast's bar. After she left town, Brubaker's paper
carried several humorous cartoons depicting the event. Even Weast,
who was clearly amused and pleased by the notoriety, found a way
to market it. When patrons arrived at the Golden Palace Saloon to
see the famous painting that the "Kansas Cyclone" tried to remove,
they were greeted by a sign outside the door:

ALL NATIONS WELCOME, EXCEPT CARRIE.

IN NEW YORK, during that same year Carrie Nation came to Peoria,
the original *Nymphs and Satyr* painting was gone. Edward "Ned"
Stokes sold off his property, including his interest in the Hoffman
House and its art. Stokes was a sick man, and doctors told him he
had only months to live. The painting that had caused such lively

conversation and controversy for many years was taken down, purchased anonymously at auction, and disappeared from sight. Stokes
died on November 2, 1901.

Stokes tried to a live a good and straight life after his tumultuous tryst with Josie Mansfield and eventual murder of Jim Fisk.
Mansfield had went away, traveling to Europe after Fisk's death
and where she stayed for many years. Following his time in prison,
Stokes put his efforts into the hotel business but was a troubled
man, haunted by the spirit of his dead nemesis. "He had gone to
bed every night with the gas at full flame and a valet on a couch,
beside him," reported *The Sun* shortly after Stokes death. "He was
always afraid of Jim Fisk's ghost."

Many years later, in 1943, the original *Nymphs and Satyr*, thought
to have vanished forever, was found tucked away and collecting
dust in a large Manhattan warehouse where it was believed to have
sat dormant for some four-plus decades. It was uncovered, revived,
and reborn. "A fabulous painting which scandalized the '80s was
seen in public last week for the first time since 1901," *Time* magazine reported. It was given a new life and admired by a different
generation of critics who understood its significance as a work of
art and its importance to New York history.

Since its revival, the painting has hung at many prestigious art
houses in New York City, including the world-renowned Metropolitan Museum of Art.

In 1934, a smaller copy of *Nymphs and Satyr* was displayed in
a Trenton, New Jersey, bar. Since at that time the original was
nowhere to be found, the bar owner was asked questions about the
gigantic painting that was once the talk of New York. "[The artist]
may have painted a second," he said, speaking of the original, "but
I can't prove it." That comment would have certainly raised a few
eyebrows in Peoria.

Unfortunately, the one man who could answer such a claim, the
painting's creator, William Bouguereau, was long gone. *Nymphs
and Satyr* would become his most famous work in America, but
whether the French artist knew, accepted, or outright dismissed its
exploits overseas is not known. Four years after Carrie Nation's visit to Peoria, in 1905, at the age of 80, Bouguereau quietly slumped

over beside his easel, paint brush in hand. He succumbed to a weak heart.

PETER WEAST died in October of 1922 at his home in Los Angeles after suffering a "brief illness," the papers reported. Even at the age of 74 and now living halfway across the country, Weast still had ties to Peoria, including several businesses and a whole block of buildings on the central location of Jefferson Street between Fulton and Main.

When Weast relocated to California, he put his valuables in storage, including the *Nymphs and Satyr* copy, which stayed in Peoria, hidden safely away in the loft of an old barn. But it wasn't there very long. Another bar owner named Robert McClugage retrieved the painting and moved it to The Annex, a popular meeting place for the city's top civic and business leaders on Jefferson Street. Just getting the large painting back into a downtown building was an almost-insurmountable task, involving extra manpower and lifts. It was placed near the entrance just off a side street, Niagara Court, where everyone could see it as they walked in.

This must have pleased Peter Weast. Even upon his death, the painting was still in his estate, and he defended its worth to the end. There was never any mention of it being a reproduction in any stories about Carrie Nation's visit to his bar. Weast treated it as a unique work of art worthy of his saloon's wall. He never questioned or apologized for the attention it gained.

Some claim that at the time of Nation's visit, Weast still had no idea the painting was a copy of the original, an argument that's difficult to believe. After all, the truth lies in the work itself. At the bottom right corner, a signature resides.

It's not William Bouguereau.

It's L.O. Kurz.

Ludwig Ferdinand Joseph Kurz von Goldenstein was born in Austria and immigrated to the United States in 1848. Born into a family of entertainers, Louis, as he was known by his parents, settled in Milwaukee, where his father, Joseph Kurz, a stage actor, directed many German-language plays. As a teen, Louis wanted to help. So he started painting scenery for his father's productions.

He was a natural artist and with a brush could recall and mimic quite beautiful reproductions of land- and seascapes. The young Kurz found work at a local newspaper and learned the art of lithography, the process of using a flat stone surface to make mass reproductions of artwork. In 1863, like most young men his age, he was mustered into the war. When his service ended, Kurz came back to Milwaukee and opened up his own lithography studio, eventually morphing into chromolithograph, which is the same process as lithography, only in color. Kurz branched out and founded the Chicago Lithograph Company, whose headquarters, along with many other businesses in the city, was destroyed by the famous fire in 1871. Undaunted, Kurz returned to Chicago in 1880 and formed a partnership with another printer named Alexander Allison. Together, they made a series of popular chromolithographs titled *Battles of the Civil War: The Complete Kurz and Allison Prints 1861-1865*. Being an accomplished artist, Kurz did all the paintings, and Allison made copies. Kurz claimed it was Abraham Lincoln who personally commissioned the paintings before his untimely death. The President wanted someone to expertly depict the battles in color, Kurz contended. Later, the work was criticized for softening the reality of war, but at the time, the prints were quite striking, garish in color, and very patriotic. They sold a ton.

How or why Kurz was interested in *Nymphs and Satyr* is not known. But for some reason he painted it. The copying of others artists' work was not an unusual practice. In fact, the process was used in teaching, especially in Paris where young artists would (and still do) set up their easels in The Louvre and recreate their favorite pieces, oftentimes as big as the piece itself. Kurz did such a good job with *Nymphs and Satyr* that many were fooled. But all they had to do was look at the bottom of the painting and see the signature of L.O. Kurz, the moniker of Ludwig Ferdinand Joseph Kurz von Goldenstein, or Louis Kurz, the lithograph painter from Chicago. They also needed to know that Kurz was not the original artist. Perhaps this was Weast's ruse. He knew, but never told.

IN THE 1950s, Peoria's stately bar, The Annex, was closed and the building sold. The new owners, a storage company, moved in. The entrance of the building was moved to a more convenient location along the busier Jefferson Street. The *Nymphs and Satyr* painting that had greeted patrons at the door for many years was covered up by a temporary wall at first, made up of loose boards over the glass. Then a more permanent wall was built. But the painting remained, shrouded from public sight for eternity, it would seem, because it was too large and too costly to move. Many years later, it was rediscovered again when the walls were torn down and the building razed.

Today, the Peoria Historical Society owns the painting, and it hangs for all to see in a downtown bar, called Richard's on Main, located in the basement of an old movie palace theater. It still garners attention and stares.

ONLY 10 years after the Peoria visit, in 1911, Carrie Nation was gone at the age of 65. Even the cause of her death was contested. Newspaper accounts say she had a nervous breakdown and dementia, but that was never proven. She became a broken and desolate woman after committing her beloved but mentally ill child Charlien to the asylum in December of 1910, an event from which Carrie never recovered. Her heart gave out soon after.

Carrie Nation would not live to see Prohibition enacted in 1920, although her footprints were all over it. Shortly before her death, she said, "I feel now that this great wave of prohibition that is sweeping over the whole land propelled by a mighty power of public sentiment, will go on and on, until national Prohibition will be the ultimate outcome."

She never admitted defeat in her efforts, as some have suggested, but when asked why she rarely used her hatchet after the stint in jail and visit to Peoria, Nation for once may have hinted at a concession. "I would have dropped from exhaustion before I had gone a block," she said.

A COLONEL FOR THE OCCASION

We love and hate the weather. Most every day we keep close watch on it, try to predict it, and in the end accept it even though we don't care for the result in many instances. When we're blindsided by adverse weather we didn't see or hear coming, we curse ourselves for not being better informed, oftentimes by our own fault or reasonably by others whose job it is to predict such things, known as forecasting. That's why every year on the days leading up to the Fourth of July holiday, we incessantly check the forecast. For on that day, more than others, most Americans will be spending a considerable amount of time outdoors. Of course we know it will be warm on that day, maybe very warm. And in some areas of the country, it will be downright hot, like in the Southwest, where it could be a scorcher. It might rain. It might pour. A storm, in fact, may produce winds that swirl together in a funnel with such force that it causes great structural damage. Or, on the coasts, wind-whipped water sucked from the ocean may come crashing violently ashore. That's the extreme, of course. Most of the time, it's just plain hot. The summer of 1776 was no different. The east was feeling the heat. So you can only imagine what it was like in June and July of that year when some 56 men from 13 states spent days packed in a room together, each in the dress of the time—heavy wool coats, long leggings, and powdered wigs—drafting and signing a document whose purpose and contents some 250 years later still bears celebration. The following story is about the next 100TH year. Not the following 100 years, but the day we celebrated the 100TH anniversary of the Declaration of Independence. On July 4, 1876, sanctioned by the government, and known as the Centennial, cities across the nation were allowed to step up celebrations with extended parades, grand speakers, and spectacular fireworks. Peoria was no exception. On that day, an esteemed gentleman and local war hero was raised high above others and gave a speech that defined a career. His story is told here from the perspective of a busy and

complicated time, filled with great highs and lows, turmoil, and inde-
cisions. 1876 was a fascinating year, as you will see, but also a worthy
representation of a nation celebrating 100 years of independence to
reflect on the past and prepare for the future, despite its unpredictability. Just like the weather.

FOR WELL over a century, scholars, journalists, and history profes-
sors have been debating and reconstructing the events that took
place near the end of June 1876 on a scenic Montana bluff in a
remote area overlooking a slow-moving, winding river known as
the Little Bighorn. It was there that a dashing West Point grad, who
had earned a reputation on the Civil War battlefields as a brave but
somewhat reckless leader, led a Cavalry division, over 200 strong,
into a famous battle against an overwhelming force of Lakota and
Cheyenne warriors. The Indians called him "Yellow Hair" due to
his strikingly long, gold-colored locks. The men called him General, even though that rank was a "brevet" rank—temporarily given
during the Civil War—and his rank on the plains was colonel. The
rest of the country adoringly knew him by his last name: Custer.

Some facts about that day are generally not questioned. Custer
and his men sat alone in unforgiving western territory surrounded
by mountains and plains and faced a relentless and brutal enemy.
An attack was imminent. In the opinion of the U.S. government,
the Indians had clearly demonstrated a lack of cooperation. The
open, largely uncharted land that stood west of the Mississippi
River and east of California was too important to ignore. Patch
by patch, bands of men would move west—not explorers *per se,* but
soldiers, scouting and fighting if necessary until the land was free
of resident peoples—"savages," to the people moving west—who
didn't buy into the plan.

It was a costly journey. Custer and his men had already seen the
remains of skirmishes gone wrong: bodies mutilated and heads
capped, their scalps ripped from the skull, cleanly, as if tearing a
stitch from a buckskin jacket.

Eight years before the Battle of the Little Bighorn, a major
named John Elliott, who was in charge of a lighter division, made
a grave and indefensible mistake. Chasing after decoy Indians, the

major's small band was soon ambushed, outnumbered, and subsequently massacred. For a time, the whereabouts of Major Elliott's command was unknown. Days passed without word or hope. They were assumed dead, but where and how? When the troops were finally found, their butchered corpses were littered across the earth like dandelions in the grass. The slaughter was quick and brutal. A major's judgment, it was determined, was obscured by impatience and pride.

You would think a young commanding officer would learn from such mistakes. After all, it was Custer and his squadron that found the bloody carnage and the major's mangled body, cut to pieces. Not so, it seemed. The Indians were shifty and tactical, but vulnerable. To win is to outwit and out-hit, despite the risk. Elliott had the right idea, Custer thought, just the wrong outcome.

This is where it gets tricky. In Custer's mind, a surprise attack was the best option. But his orders were to wait until other divisions that were pursuing the Lakota and Cheyenne moved into desirable positions; then, and only then, could an advance on the enemy be achieved with maximum efficiency. The general waited reluctantly, mostly on horseback. Then a scout arrived with disturbing news. An enemy camp had been spotted along a nearby river. The trail of many ponies confirmed it. Is this what Elliott faced and lost? Never one to dwell on past regressions and eager to proceed, Custer made a fateful decision. No regrets.

He would pounce like a lion on a wounded gazelle.

As MIDNIGHT approached the city of Peoria on July 3, 1876, dark clouds opened up and a heavy rain fell. Most of the city went to sleep, the papers noted, and "prepared to bear the disappointment [of their absence] as best they could." But a few stragglers stayed up late. Bravely, several members of the Veteran Light Guard, muskets in hand, ducked under the cover of a window awning and waited for the magical hour to arrive.

"When the clocks announced the birth of the second century of our great republic," the *Peoria Daily Transcript* reported, "some adventuresome souls, whom water could not scare, gathered in the street and tried, amid the mud, to explode damp firecrackers and shoot wet guns." Scant sounds of muffled pops and a volley of cracks from the Guard's water-logged muskets celebrated the start of the nation's Centennial. "What we will do and how we shall do it," the papers proclaimed in announcing preparations for the 100TH Fourth of July. A busy day was planned, filled with grand festivals, marches, speeches, and fireworks. And all with the government's stamp of approval, of course.

But it wasn't as easy a sell as you might think. In Washington, D.C., a year earlier, in planning for the Centennial, Congressmen extolled the virtues of a country united in celebration. That was never in question. After all, Fourth of July festivities until then had been mostly subdued affairs filled with long-winded speakers and politicians reminding the masses how important the day was. A band played, a few fireworks popped, nothing extraordinary. But a Centennial celebration would be different, more spectacular and more important. Lawmakers set out to support and fund it, allowing states and cities to plan like no other Fourth of July holiday in the past. The government's showcase would be a Centennial exposition in Philadelphia, a massive undertaking of time and money. It seemed like a snap to pass. But like most proposals in the political arena, there was dissension. In question was whether or not to spend public funds on such displays. Several House members stood up in support, including Illinois' Democrat Carter Harrison of Chicago. "The national anthem will swell," Harrison eloquently stated in chambers, "and, as it goes westward until reaching a line stretching from far north to the extreme south on the Gulf of Mexico, one grand peal shall be heard, a peal of a thousand guns, rocking the very foundations of the earth." In the end, political bickering over finances weren't enough to refute a call for commemorations nationally and in individual cities, if they wished. The celebration-planning committees could commence. Congress approved. The Centennial would truly be a special day for America.

And who didn't want to celebrate? The Centennial year was coming at the end of a pivotal and disruptive period in American history, but hope was afoot. Scars left by the Civil War, now 11 years removed, were slowly healing and Reconstruction, still a work in progress, was helping bridge the gap between a fractured nation.

The Stride of the Century depicting the Centennial of the United States, lithograph by Currier & Ives c. 1876. Print courtesy the Library of Congress.

THE STRIDE OF A CENTURY.

In retrospect, the year 1876 is considered by many historians to be the final year of the Reconstruction era, in part, because that's the year—thanks to the presidential elections—when the Old South lost its voice and a New South emerged that was more transparent and more allied with a nation as a whole to solve its problems.

But it was a volatile mix of forces. The expansion to the west and innovations like the transcontinental railroads were changing the landscape in a positive direction, but there was also deep corruption. Farmers burdened by debt got squeezed and corporations, mainly the railroad companies, emerged, driven by owners who lined their pockets at the expense of landowners and with help from shady government bank loans. Many black citizens, former slaves aspiring for a better life, were abandoned by principles that set them free. Reconstruction, many reasoned, was a dark page in the saga of American history. Now it was coming to an end.

Soon the Gilded Age would begin, replacing Reconstruction with an explosion of growth and industry, a demand for more production, expanding transportation, and, as it turned out, great wealth for some. But that would be in the decade ahead, the beginning of the next 100 years. 1876 would be the bridge. A pivotal year, for sure. But at the time, for most Americans, it was the Centennial year, a milestone in the nation's history. A time to celebrate, not wallow, was the thinking. To look ahead and begin a new century with a hopeful resolve. For those who could see through the hazy past, outstanding prospects for a growing and emerging nation were at hand.

When the sun rose in Peoria on July 4, the overnight storms were gone, and the rain was light and intermittent. Efforts were made to adjust the schedule to meet the demands of the weather, but hopes ran high that the day's activities would proceed as planned. Already, festive crowds were lining the streets.

The crowds were anticipating a day of parades and speeches. The military would be proudly on display, mostly marching units and veterans of wars. But despite the vast amount of weaponry and firepower on hand, the finely coifed soldiers were mostly for show. The only men in the country seeing or seeking any combat action were hundreds of miles away in the Western Theater, engaged in "operations against the hostile Sioux."

By morning's light, dignitaries, honored guests, and soldiers began to gather on North Jefferson Street. Promptly at nine, they marched. Military divisions and artillery units stepped side-by-side with local groups and organizations. Among them were the Lodge brothers, Benevolent Society members, and the Brotherhood of Locomotive Engineers. "The wagons exhibiting the different manufactures and trades were very novel," the *Transcript* reported.

The Spring Lake Ice Company, the Burdett Organ Shop, the Wilson Sewing Machine Factory, and Kirkman Brooms were some of the businesses on hand, each displaying and demonstrating its wares. "The process of making brooms was very interesting," a reporter enthused, "as very few people had before seen a broom factory in operation."

The L.B. Bigham carriage manufacturer displayed three large wagons, one of which carried three lighter-load wagons. The running gears were painted red, white, and blue. The city butchers were on hand too, riding horseback with red aprons and white sashes. The Mason's wagon consisted of "a bevy of little girls, handsomely dressed." On the side of the wagon was the inscription, "We visit the sick, bury the dead and educate the orphans."

The decorations throughout the city were fine. "The whole length of Adams and Washington Street were trimmed with green trees and flags, and Bridge Street was a mass of foliage." A triple arch stretched across Adams at Main with evergreens and flowers entwined on each side to spell *July 4 1776* and *July 4 1876*. In the middle arch were the words *Liberty and Union,* formed by golden letters. Small flags could be counted "by the thousands" and "festoons of oak leaves interspersed with flags" adorned several downtown buildings.

The Chamber of Commerce Building on Washington "had a picture of Liberty, draped with the same material, displayed in the front." Seven locomotives were drawn along the tracks on Water Street, as the *Peoria Daily Transcript* defined: "The engines were most beautifully decked with flowers and flags, and having in different places, ladies and children draped in different costumes as statuary." The parade mass, nearly two miles in length, took 30 minutes to pass a given point. "The finest seen since the war," the paper exclaimed. The end of the parade was Darst's Groves, a garden area at the head of Jackson Street where the procession disbanded and the crowds gathered to hear the ceremonies. A prayer was followed by the reading of the Declaration of Independence. The honored reciter was a man named L.W. James. "In a clear measured voice," the *Daily Transcript* reported, "he read line after line of that glorious document, only pausing during the bursts of frequent applause."

William Cockle, the president of the Centennial committee, briefly quieted the crowd. "I have the pleasure of introducing to you the greatest speaker east or west of the Allegany Mountains, or anywhere else," he said. The applause started up again as a portly, slightly balding man with one hand tugging his suit jacket lapel sauntered onstage. He was no stranger to Peorians.

"Colonel Robert Ingersoll," Cockle shouted as the crowd cheered.

The guest speaker was indeed Col. Robert G. Ingersoll, a local lawyer turned war hero, who wasted no time in rousing the crowd with a tribute to the Declaration: "You have just heard the grandest, the bravest, and the profoundest political document that was ever signed by man," he bellowed.

Ingersoll was the perfect fit for Peoria's Centennial Celebration and anticipation had been running high. Whether he could make it on time was another matter. Ingersoll had just wrapped up as guest speaker of the contentious and exhausting Republican national convention in Cincinnati, Ohio. He returned home to Peoria for rest, but he soon set off again, this time to an engagement in New York. He kept sending telegrams back to Peoria that he would be there for the ceremonies, and the papers anxiously kept tabs. Late on July 3, Ingersoll arrived by train. He retired to his newly built four-story mansion, tired but back at home. Although he was still weary from his travels, he arrived at the podium as scheduled the next day.

Ingersoll was just beginning to gain notoriety as a public speaker. Born in Dresden, New York, the son of an ardent abolitionist preacher, Ingersoll as a teen was schooled in downstate Illinois and came to Peoria in 1857, where he began a law practice. Along with his brother Clark, also a lawyer, Ingersoll opened a small office on North Adams Street in Peoria that served as a makeshift bedroom for Robert, who slept on the lobby couch at night while his newly married brother and bride retired to a cramped apartment nearby. Together, they worked railroad litigation but eventually were asked to defend criminal cases. Ingersoll liked the more demanding work for better pay. After winning a perjury case for a "wealthy" man, they were rewarded "six city lots worth at least two hundred and fifty dollars apiece" for their efforts. Ingersoll remarked to his brother, "I think we are going to make lots of money." They did. But the rest of the country was suffering.

In the summer of 1857, due to corrupt railroad handlings, land grants, and the overextension of manufacturing loans, the nation went into severe recession—in fact, depression. A large trust company defaulted, and the markets panicked. Ingersoll didn't feel the pinch, but watched as destitution turned to desperation. For many, the only respite was the church. "The Christian Churches of the land are now in the midst of an extraordinary awakening," declared *Harpers Weekly*. Churches were packed with rejected and downtrodden souls who turned to God for help—and spiritual guidance. Ingersoll was ambivalent, but supportive. He understood the great weight of the issue and longed for the day when economic conditions would improve and people would "stop praying and go to preying." Clearly a lawyer speaking.

LEFT: Robert G. Ingersoll. Photograph courtesy the Library of Congress.

TOP: Ingersoll in 1861, colonel of the Illinois Eleventh Calvary, based in Peoria. Photograph courtesy the Local History and Genealogy Collection, Peoria Public Library, Peoria, IL.

Ingersoll's upbringing would suggest he was a deeply religious man like his father, but the church was a chore to him. He found a true passion in literature and history books instead. This did not mean he was a "godless" man, as one biographer points out. He often invoked God's name in letters asking for blessings or divine praise. Still, in regards to the depression and the resulting spread of religious rebirth across the country, his actions and words were more sympathetic than spiritual. (Later, his agnostic views on religion would define him.)

Instead, Ingersoll turned to politics to help those looking for redemption. He followed campaigns closely and used his success as an attorney to influence others he supported, like fellow lawyer and statesman Stephen Douglas. Ingersoll was against slavery, but like Douglas believed the principles lied in the individual states' right to choose. In 1858, the Democrats of the Fifth Congressional District nominated Ingersoll for representative to Congress. He lost the election but gained supporters with his impassioned speeches. Ingersoll also blamed a zealous editor of the mostly Republican Peoria newspaper the *Transcript* for besmirching his reputation. The paper falsely accused Ingersoll of being "drunk, profane, licentious and vulgar" during a debate. They quoted an "observer," who claimed the speaker (Ingersoll) was so inebriated that he "several times fell partially off the stand." Ingersoll knew the paper had embellished the facts and sought to correct it. He met the editor in the street and demanded an apology. The only account of their meeting comes from the editor, who accused Ingersoll of "vengeance," claiming "he [Ingersoll] would whip us if we opened our mouth to him, ordering us to move on, and applying to us various forcible but we must admit, rather intelligent epithets." In the end, the paper's remarks did not hurt Ingersoll in Peoria. As a local candidate, he won the city's support by votes, as did Douglas over Lincoln, but the rest of the state sided with the national debate on slavery, which Lincoln won. Ingersoll would find his next challenge in the war.

Just a few weeks after the attack on Fort Sumter, on April 22, 1861, Ingersoll wrote Illinois Governor Richard Yates asking to form a regiment in Peoria. "Will you accept?" he asked. The Governor did and the Illinois Eleventh Cavalry was born. The *Transcript,* now on friendly terms with Ingersoll, proclaimed: "This regiment is intended to be one of the best in service." Ingersoll would serve as Colonel.

Not everything went as planned. The early regiments were poorly equipped and often neglected. The men drilled at Camp Lyon in Peoria, the present site of Glen Oak Park, and grew restless with each passing day. Oftentimes, some of the more adventurous types broke the tedium by scaling the camp's walls and perusing the city for recreation. Some never returned. Ingersoll was unfazed. He sternly commanded those who obeyed orders and patiently waited. Then, on March 9, 1862, nearly a year after being formed, the company bid farewell to Illinois and headed to St. Louis, worn coats on their backs but freshly armed. They were headed to battle, somewhere. In St Louis, they boarded several steamers and joined General Grant's troops in Pittsburg Landing, Tennessee. The first shots they heard came from a small church called Shiloh.

Ingersoll and his men spent the next two days in skirmishes, but lost only four men. The Union considered Shiloh a win. The Battle of Cornith was next, and the Illinois Eleventh fought valiantly, earning a fine reputation as "wild-cats" for engaging guerrilla factions of the Confederate army. And so it went for months. Battle after battle, skirmish after skirmish, until Ingersoll, who was committed to his troops, became weary of the travails of combat. "The sooner the war closes," he wrote home, "the better I shall be pleased."

That December, Ingersoll's military service abruptly came to an end. During the Battle of Lexington, he fell off his charging horse and was captured. Thanks to a prisoner exchange, Ingersoll spent only a few days in custody. He used that time to entertain fellow prisoners and captors who demanded a "speech, speech" from the emerging orator. Propping up a box, he stood on it and addressed the curious on both sides of the conflict, who listened together as if there was no animosity between them. After his release and injured by the fall from the horse, Ingersoll asked to be mustered out. He was granted release.

Ingersoll came back to Peoria with honors, served as the appointed Illinois Attorney General for two years, and opened up a successful law practice. During the war, he also found time to marry a local girl from nearby Groveland.

In 1876, Ingersoll became known nationally for his stirring speeches about the war, Reconstruction, and politics. His views on religion were also getting notice. Ingersoll did not shy away from his thoughts on the subject, oftentimes belittling religious beliefs. "The church cannot touch, cannot crush, cannot stare, cannot stop or stay me," he once lectured. But his more-mainstream views on freedom and the sanctity of the family would resonate with the masses, and his speeches, sometimes three hours long, delivered almost always from memory, were riveting. Mark Twain, in his usual whimsical way, said of one of Ingersoll's talks, "It was the supreme combination of English words that was ever put together since the world began." Twain's praise reverberated. Ingersoll would later be recognized "as one of the country's great orators."

In May of 1876, when the city of Peoria announced formal plans for a large and grand Centennial spectacle in the streets, the emphasis would be on the military and remembering the war dead. Even the site of the stage was moved from the courthouse square—a typical place for large gatherings—to Darst's Groves so it would be symbolically closer to a cemetery. The city boasted: "In the year of our Lord, in the year of independence 100, Peoria, the Central City of Illinois, will celebrate the Centennial Anniversary of the nation's independence in an extensive and magnificent manner, never before known in the city or excelled by any other city in the west." When it came time to pick an esteemed speaker for the event, the choice was obvious. Not only was Robert Ingersoll a fine speechmaker, but he was a military man to boot. Known by his close friends as "Bob," most others called him "The Colonel." Ingersoll eagerly accepted the appellation.

Throughout the lengthy but stirring speech, Ingersoll repeated the question, "And what more did these men do?", referring to the Founding Fathers. He then followed with an explanation of their importance: "They laid down the doctrine that governments were instituted among men for the purpose of preserving the rights of the people," he thundered.

"I thank every one of them from the bottom of my heart that they did sign it. I thank them for their courage—for their patriotism—for their wisdom—for their splendid confidence in themselves and in the human race. I thank them for what they were and what we are—for what they did and for what we have received—for what they suffered, and for what we enjoy."

Ingersoll had no trouble evoking a swell of patriotism from the appreciative crowd, but despite the pageantry and nationalism of the Centennial, politically, 1876 was no celebratory year. It was a presidential election year and the nation was split between two men, both governors, with similar views on reform but with deeply divided support. Republican Rutherford B. Hayes, a Whig lawyer who became governor of Ohio, was favored by Northerners and hard-line Republicans, but he was despised by the majority of white

Southerners who still blamed the Republicans for the war. Their choice was Samuel J. Tilden, the Democratic governor of New York. Outgoing was the current two-term president, a Civil War veteran and esteemed general who still held that title, even in the White House. General Grant was anxious to leave.

Ingersoll, now a staunch Republican, reluctantly backed Hayes. But it was not his first choice. James G. Blaine, a fiery but moderate Republican, had his backing. Blaine was the "acid-tongued" Congressman from Maine who still harbored deep resentments toward the South, the war, and Reconstruction in general. The Republicans were split between three factions: those who supported the outgoing president, Grant, called the Stalwarts; the anti-Grant camp, or Mugwumps; and the Halfbreeds, or followers of Blaine, like Ingersoll.

Ingersoll's nomination speech for Blaine at the Republican convention in June is still considered a highlight of the orator's illustrious career. A writer from the *Chicago Tribune* called it "impassioned, artful, brilliant and persuasive." Conceding the weakness of his after-the-moment account, the *Tribune* reporter wrote, "The matchless method of the man can never be imagined in type. To realize the prodigious force, the inexpressible power, the irrestrainable fervor of the audience requires actual sight." Ingersoll's words, he continued, "swept the whole body like a tumultuous flood."

Ingersoll concluded his convention speech with a flourish: "In the name of the great republic, the only republic that ever existed upon the face of the earth; in the name of all her defenders and all of her supporters; in the name of all her soldiers living; in the name of her soldiers that died upon the field of battle; and in the name of those that perished in the skeleton clutch of famine at Andersonville and Libby, whose sufferings he so vividly remembers—Illinois—Illinois nominates for the next president of this country that prince of parliamentarians, that leader of leaders, James G. Blaine."

It didn't work.

Although Blaine got most of the first-ballot votes, it wasn't enough. The next day, two of the five candidates dropped out, throwing their backers' support mostly to Hayes' camp. When New York went for Hayes, victory was in hand. Blaine was gracious in defeat.

James G. Blaine. Photo-
graph courtesy the Library
of Congress.

After the convention, Ingersoll put his support behind the party
and did stump speeches on behalf of Hayes. But in Peoria, on July 4,
he kept political preferences in check and commended the virtues
of a nation, as a whole, on its 100TH birthday. "Deafening was the
applause that greeted him," the *Daily Transcript* reported, "and
it was only when tired out, and they could applaud no more that
the crowd would allow him to proceed."

NATIONALLY, FESTIVITIES to mark the Centennial anniversary
began on the first day of the first month of the New Year. On January 1, 1876, in Philadelphia, the birthplace of the Constitution,

the party got off to a rousing start. At the stroke of midnight, military men marched, rifles were fired in the air, and bells tolled. A bell ringer in the steeple tolled out 1-7-7-6, 1-8-7-6, then began a peal in which the bells of all the city's churches joined for a tribute to the shrine of liberty. "A tremendous roar waved through the streets as pistol shots and exploding firecrackers drowned out the first bars of 'The Star Spangled Banner,'" the papers reported.

In other cities, like Peoria, the start to the Centennial year was rather plain in ceremony and reflective in tone. 1875 was nothing special, but it was another year removed from the dogma of war. Municipalities across the country were rebuilding or, in Peoria's case, building out. "Slow and steady progress," the city pronounced on New Year's Day. "Nearly 100 buildings had been built the previous year." A new courthouse, hotel, and opera house were in the works. "The next few months will surely see them both under way, if not completed." Another building, an auditorium, was appropriately named Centennial Hall. It would be used exclusively to house events and welcome guest speakers.

The sign of the times was in the ads that peppered the pages of the newspaper. Products of all varieties and needs were being pressed upon the public with promises to "buy cheaper and feel better" in the coming year. "Pure wine and liquors for medical purposes" was offered up by a local druggist, along with a daily special on "fine toilet soap." Burning oils for lamps and headlights were for sale that burned more brilliantly, lasted longer, and were "the safest in the world," the ads proclaimed. And anyone who bought a carriage or buggy from the Foilz, Gentes Co. was given "special attention to repairs," if needed, of course. The conditions of the streets were of special concern. "Those interested in locomotion on our streets," the *Peoria Daily Transcript* implied, "may look through the coming months of the year just dawned, hoping to see some street paving done before its close."

The first day of 1876 was a dreary one. "Midnight bells sounded out a glad welcome," the *Transcript* reported. Then "the rain poured down, the wind blew and the mud was outrageous." There were speeches and private dinners but hardly any public display of celebration for the start of the Centennial year. The weather was just too unbearable. "The wind came whistling through our streets," the paper reported. "At city hall, the flag which hung at the head of the staff was [ripped] and borne away by the wind." A large window pane at the post office "went in with a crash" and building awnings were ripped from their moors and strewn about the streets.

Despite the gloomy weather, there was optimism. The newspaper's attitude, however, was somewhat incredulous. The end of the first 100 years had been marred by a bloody, disruptive, and costly war that the nation was still reeling from financially, emotionally, and physically. Reconstruction was still in flux and a Union general had just served two terms as president. The South was now demanding their voice be heard—right up to the White House door. Homelessness and helping the poor and destitute were some of the hotbed issues of the time, even in Peoria. "The day was rife for speculation," the *Transcript* editorialized after announcing the city's "many projects and improvements" for the upcoming year. "But to leave speculation and come to reality again. We must notice the New Year's Dinner at Grace Mission (to feed the homeless, orphaned and widowed).

"An uncommonly large number were present," the paper added ominously.

For some, the Centennial celebrations would be a necessary and needed diversion. But on New Year's Day in Peoria, no plans were discussed publically how the city would celebrate the actual Centennial holiday in July. That would come later.

That was not the case, however, in Philadelphia.

By the start of 1876, preparations were long since underway for the Philadelphia Centennial Exhibition, the first World's Fair in the United States. "The most remarkable event that would happen in their lifetime," Philadelphians were told. But they would not be alone. On May 10, Opening Day, people arrived in droves and from all corners of the country and globe. More than eight million showed up that summer to walk the winding pathways, visit the large pavilions, explore the industry and progress halls, and view startling new inventions. These included Alexander Graham Bell's telephone, which, as it turned out, attracted less attention than packaged magic tricks. The city was bursting with patriotic pride that led right up to the official Centennial celebration that July. "Building after building comes into view, and soon the panorama is before you," recorded one visitor who rode by train from Peoria to Philadelphia's Centennial Station. "The magnitude of the enterprise bursts upon you at once and you cannot realize that such a gigantic world's fair is actually in progress, and yet there it is." Then, on July 4, during a stifling heat wave with temperatures near 90 degrees, 50,000 invited guests filled Independence Square while another 100,000 packed the surrounding streets. Newly nominated presidential candidate Hayes was there along with several Civil War generals, among them William Tecumseh Sherman. "There in an effervescent of parades and encampments, of excitement, effort, and confident expectation," a historian wrote, "was the essence of the Republic."

Most notable was the number of women who were marching in parades. The Centennial Exhibition had given birth to the Women's Centennial Committee, and the Women's Pavilion was their creation. The building itself was a monumental achievement, although it stood, quite symbolical some thought, with two large cannons strategically pointing at its front walls. Only in the works for several months, male counterparts said it couldn't be built in time. They gravely underestimated the will of a movement.

With little political support and inspired by the significance of the holiday, the Women's Suffrage Association decided to write their own version of the Declaration of Independence, which included equal representation. Founder Susan B. Anthony delivered a short message in Philadelphia on July 4, although not by choice of the planning committee. She barged through the crowd, nudged her way to the podium, and briefly disrupted the proceedings. After being politely received, she said a few brief words before walking through the crowd and handing out the revised document to "stretched hands," mostly men, who stood on chairs to get a copy. "From that day the phrase 'male supremacy' had a hollow ring," was one writer's assessment.

Nothing so heavy or radical was on display in Peoria that July day. Ingersoll's speech was moving but not confrontational. He was, as usual, the papers noted, "Forcible, witty, original and positive." But above all, he was patriotic. In the speech, however, were flourishes about religion and its role in politics, which today would be regarded as controversial: "The first secular government; the first government that said every church has exactly the same rights and no more; every religion has the same rights, and no more. In other words, our fathers were the first men who had the sense, had the genius, to know that no church should be allowed to have a sword." Ingersoll stated that most European nations were still based on the union between religion and state. "Recollect this," he said, claiming the writers of the Constitution had founded "the first secular government ever in the world."

After the dedications and speeches, more lighthearted fare, like shirtless men jousting on unstable boats–regally titled "Naval Engagement"–kept the crowds entertained. A regatta boat race became comical only by default. There were so many pleasure boats on the river, the papers reported, that no one knew which boats were part of the race. And a swimming match was held, won by a man named Mendenhall who covered the 300-yard course in 3 minutes and 15 seconds. At night, Chinese lanterns were hung out on the streets, and the courthouse square was lined by colorful decorative lights placed every ten feet.

After dark, the crowds started to gather along Hamilton Street to witness the fireworks display. At 9 PM, the bursting of rockets and the "colored balls of fire" from the Roman Candles lit up the night sky. Due to weather, many of the rockets were waterlogged and "worthless." Some were so damp they wouldn't ignite. "Hardly had the display begun," the papers noted, "when pattering rain drops drove the multitude home in haste, but not until they all disappeared did the fireworks close." In the end, only about half were set off. The finest-looking display, the papers described, was a static ornament of sparking lights depicting George Washington on horseback with hat raised high. It received the most applause.

In the end, the city's festivities were marred by only minor mishaps. "It is not supposed the Fourth of July could pass without somebody being hurt," the *Daily Transcript* reported. But despite the firepower on display that day, the number of serious accidents was few. One boy named George Pickney, the son of a reverend, was hit in the back by a sky rocket that "instead of rising in the air, started in a horizontal direction." The boy was knocked "senseless," but recovered. Another teenage boy was seriously injured after being struck by ball shot from a revolver by a man who claims he aimed into the crowd by accident when the gun went off. "Instead of shooting blank cartridges, as any man of sense would do," the papers chided, "he shot ball." Still, the day was full of pomp and celebration as revelers who braved the rain were treated to "a Centennial Fourth, the grandest ever witnessed in Peoria."

An editorial in the *Daily Transcript* summed it up:

"Year by year, so long as the republic endures, the day should be commemorated. On the Centennial anniversary of the birth of the Republic we should put aside our self-glorification of our progress during the century, should suspend our references to material progress in territorial extent, in physical wealth and in aesthetic culture, and turn our head's backwards to the men who by their act cemented the growing feeling of the people of the colonies and created a new nation, as it were, out of nothing. They are entitled to that honor."

"WHOOP-LA!" the headlines read victoriously. "One Hundred Fourths of July in One."

But the euphoria was short-lived.

The next day, July 5, was startlingly different.

ON THAT day, in cities throughout much of the nation, word was finally leaking out that the Seventh U.S. Cavalry stationed at a remote fort in the western landscape of the Black Hills had been soundly beaten by Lakota and Cheyenne warriors near the Little Bighorn River. "General Custer attacked the Indians," the first telegraph message read before delivering the sickening news of the outcome, including the shocking fate of the "Boy General" himself. William Tecumseh Sherman, the veteran Commanding General of the U.S. Army, received the first dispatches announcing the battle's outcome. His skepticism was apparent. It must be exaggerated, he thought. A field general wouldn't be so imprudent as to attack such a large number of Indians, was his first reaction.

General George A. Custer.
Photograph courtesy the
Library of Congress.

Who would be so brazen to defy orders? Sherman hoped the initial dispatches were wrong. He questioned the action of his top commander on the battlefield and waited for more details. It got worse.

The attack had actually occurred on June 25, but information traveled slowly back then. A rider on horseback had to get the dispatch to the nearest telegraph depot before it could be distributed to the rest of the nation. Peoria got the news on July 4, nine days after "Custer's Last Stand," and it appeared in the paper the next day. Larger Eastern cities, like Boston and New York, received the news on July 6. Sherman received the official word in a Philadelphia hotel room. The initial reports on July 4 were skeptical in his mind. Then a telegram arrived from his trusted right-hand man, General Phillip Sheridan. "Custer had a fight with the Indians and was killed," it read in part. There was no denying it now. On July 8, Sherman transcribed a letter to President Grant: "The recent reports touching the disaster which befell the 7TH Regular Cavalry led by General Custer in person are believed to be true," he wrote. Grant was livid. Custer was "reckless," in his opinion, and had a reputation for disobeying commands. "Send someone other than Custer," Grant wrote the Secretary of War several months before the engagement. But the "Boy General" could not be contained. In the end, Grant called the massacre "wholly unnecessary" and blamed Custer directly for the soldiers' deaths. The rest of the nation, however, didn't see it from a field general's perspective.

Academy of Music Building, Peoria, IL, formally Centennial Hall. Photograph courtesy the Peoria Historical Society Collection/Bradley University.

Custer was a national celebrity who was, as one writer put it, "adored by women, admired by most men, and tolerated by his few enemies." The impact of his death was immediate and extraordinary. Newspapers carried special editions for several days until the full story had been told. It was worse than imagined. Nearly half the entire Seventh Cavalry, more than 200 men, had been wiped out by the Indians. A correspondent for the *Helena Herald* described it this way: "The battleground looked like a slaughter pen, as it really was, being in a narrow ravine. The dead were very much mutilated. The situation is serious."

Due to the delay in delivery and Sherman's insistence not to make a formal announcement until he was convinced of its outcome, on July 4, Centennial Day, most of the nation had not yet heard of Custer's devastating defeat. A day of celebrations would not be marred by the awful news, but the tragedy itself would set the tone for the rest of the Centennial year.

In November were the presidential elections.

As PREDICTED, it was a close race. The two candidates, both governors, Samuel Tilden and Rutherford B. Hayes, were running neck and neck and everyone knew it. On the morning of November 7, the day after the polls closed, most of the major newspapers called it: "Tilden wins a tight one!" Unlike the infamous *Chicago Tribune* headline mistake, "Dewey Defeats Truman," that would occur many years later, the Tilden victory was substantiated, or so they thought. Tilden captured the swing states, the Electoral College, and it appeared the popular vote as well. But Republicans accused the Democrats of intimidating and bribing African-Americans—many of them former slaves—into not voting or preventing them from voting at all. The Republicans had a trump card: mostly Northern support and control of federal troops in the Southern states. The fate of the elections hung in the balance for several months and dragged on right up to the end of the calendar year.

"The year is dead, long live the year," proclaimed the *Peoria Daily Transcript*, echoing the mood of Americans on the final day of 1876, a celebratory year with an indecisive ending.

Two months into the New Year, the political impasse in Washington finally reached a conclusion. "The presidency cannot and must not be the subject of dicker and barter," argued William Wheeler, Hayes' running mate. But that's exactly what happened. With the help of a bipartisan Congressional commission, a truce was reached that became known as the Compromise of 1877, which gave Hayes the White House while restoring the South's dignity. The troops would leave the Southern states, and Hayes would appoint a Southerner to his cabinet, among other things.

IN PEORIA, expectations for the upcoming year were mixed. The paper boasted that the city had been "free of epidemics" during the preceding year and "escaped any serious disaster." Streets had been improved and "tasty" residences built. The outlook for a new hotel was "elusive and still in expectation," but construction of a new public hall was underway. The Centennial Hall, which housed many of the rousing speeches and events during 1876, was now "out of date and inappropriate," the papers declared, referring to its title. The Centennial was over and hence, the building should have a new name. At the stroke of midnight on January 1, 1877, it officially became the Academy of Music.

Ingersoll, as it turned out, became a national sensation. Based on his talk at the Republican convention and his Centennial speech in Peoria, Ingersoll the speaker was in high demand. Shortly after the July 4 celebrations, he embarked on a lecture tour and enthralled audiences with his words. His speeches became benchmarks for his lengthy career as an orator. A passage known as *Visions of War* delivered in Indianapolis in front of Civil War veterans and widows was one of his most impassioned and personal: "We see the pale cheeks of women, and the flushed faces of men," he said, referring to the audience, "and in those assemblages we see the dead whose dust we have covered with flowers." Ingersoll returned home to Peoria from his tour in September and received a large reception in his honor. But he would not stay for long. Ingersoll's friend, James Blaine, the defeated presidential candidate, asked "Bob" to stump on behalf of the party in the upcoming elections. His speeches got raves. Soon, Ingersoll was doing more traveling than lawyering and his Peoria practice suffered. He missed his family back home and made plans for them to join him permanently in Washington, D.C. They moved from Peoria in 1877.

CUSTER WAS buried with honors at West Point in October of 1877, more than a year after the bloody battle at Little Bighorn. By then, his legacy, rather than his actions on that fateful day, was cemented and revered. If he had lived, many thought, he might have faced a court martial. But for most Americans, he remained a fallen war hero. His death came at a time when patriotic pride was at center stage. Even his troops were anticipating a rousing celebration when the battle ended. As they paced forward to impending doom, one soldier blithely asked what they were all going to do once the campaign ended. "Custer will take us all with him to the Centennial," a soldier shouted.

The rest of the men laughed and cheered.

CHURCH BUILD IN A DAY

In Washington, D.C., there is no single Civil War monument, like there is the Vietnam's Veterans Memorial ("The Wall") or the more recent National World War II Memorial, which was dedicated and opened to the public in 2004. Instead, there are nearly 20 Civil War statues spread throughout the central and northwest side of the city depicting mostly generals standing tall or astride a bounding horse. All are proud Union men but one, General Albert Pike, is a Confederate. He is depicted in civilian clothes as a freemason, not a soldier of war. There is no mention of his military service. In addition to his magnificent Memorial, Abraham Lincoln is represented by the Emancipation or "Freedman" Monument, a controversial piece which depicts Lincoln standing tall as the "great emancipator" beside a shirtless and shackled slave kneeling at the President's feet. Frederick Douglass stirred up the racially insensitive debate when, as keynote speaker of the statue's dedication in 1876, he referred to the slave's submissive position and brazenly said, "A more manly attitude would have been indicative of freedom." Two statues in D.C. depict the women's role in the Civil War, including *Nuns on the Battlefield,* a large, rectangular piece shaped like a grave marker, that upon its bronze slab in the middle, 12 nuns in their traditional habits are walking together in a line. On either side of the stone are two bronze statues, one depicting the angel of patriotism and the other the angel of peace. The inscription reads: "They comforted the dying, nursed the wounded, carried hope to the imprisoned, and gave in His name a drink of water to the thirsty." After the war ended and during the Reconstruction years, Congress was on a monument-building frenzy. They commissioned most of the works and spared no expense in cost and size. Many cities throughout the nation followed suit. They also commissioned works, mostly sphere-shaped monuments that stood tall and were erected in town squares or in front of city courthouses. The tale of Peoria's first tribute to the Civil War follows. The man who came to dedicate it is one of the generals bronzed in Washington, forever sitting upon a striding horse with his long, droopy mustache appropriately blowing in the breeze. But as monuments go in Peoria, perhaps there is one remembered for its simplicity rather than any particular detail. It was neither an engraved stone nor a posturing statue. However, its symbolism was clear. It's long gone now, but the day it was built is what is remembered here—a special day and one year when even the solemn ceremonies of the dead couldn't hold back the spirit of the living.

A LONE hammer fell with a mighty bang; the crowd of "thousands" let out a joyous roar. The first nail had been driven righteously into board. Soon a volley of arms swung down furiously, each strike a quickening of the next until it sounded "like an infantry regiment firing at will," the papers reported. Ashley J. Elliott, the mastermind behind this volunteer army of builders, was one of the hammer men.

A man of faith who served the Peoria Christian Church as headmaster of the Bible class, Elliott was born in Evansville, Indiana, and moved to Peoria in 1891 to work on the railroad, a lifelong passion. He had a good reputation in town as a solid worker and thinker and was helpful in the church, organizing social gatherings and serving at meetings. On a business trip to Indianapolis, Elliott met with an Episcopal rector who had an interesting story to tell. He explained that the men of his parish had built a church addition in a day—on Thanksgiving Day, to be exact. Elliott was intrigued. The Christian Church back home was in desperate need of a new chapel on the city's West Bluff. But time and funds were lacking. He had an idea and immediately wrote to his Bible students in Peoria. Within a few days, the plan—or "scheme," as the papers called it—was set. On May 30, 1910, at 7 AM, with the sound of hammer against nail, Elliott's plan became reality. "Peorians will witness the unusual spectacle of seeing nearly one hundred churchmen, under the direction of fifty carpenters, building a church in one day," the *Peoria Journal-Transcript* reported.

The work actually began in earnest a day earlier when the formwork for the foundation was laid and the chimney bricks set. The lumber was brought in by horse carts and laid side-by-side in large piles. A temporary bleacher and stand were built. Telephone companies donated lines "free of charge" in the worker and dining tents, and a new automobile garage described as being just a few yards from the site would be used for shelter if the skies opened up. Weather was a concern but not a deterrent. There would be no delay or schedule change. Elliott was adamant that the work commence—and conclude, of course—in a single day.

At first, Elliott struggled to find the right date. Inspired by the Indiana church building on Thanksgiving, he figured a holiday would be perfect. Since the plan was already in motion, the next available holiday on the calendar would have to do. In this case, that date was Decoration Day, or Memorial Day, traditionally held on the last Monday in May. Of course, it was only circumstantial, but Elliott may have been dispirited by the choice at first. Memorial Day, a day set aside to honor the war dead, was more sobering than celebratory. He did not want to seem disrespectful. There were reasons to leave a holiday with such reverence and significance alone. The more he thought about it, however, the more he liked the idea.

Memorial Day was a national holiday filled with parades and speeches, but it was also a day set aside for communal gatherings and solemn prayer. If Elliott's thinking was correct, a church building accompanying other more-formal commemorations and dedications that day would be worthy of attention and crowds, which he was hoping for, but it would carry spiritual implications as well. His religious convictions were apparent. As a way of ending a day that was set aside to honor those who sacrificed their lives for God and country, an evening service in a church built in a single day would be an inspiration to the congregation and community. It was not a monument of stone, Elliott thought, but a house of wood and bricks that would stand as a symbol of strength and determination, like the soldiers that bravely fought in the Civil War. Yes, Elliott told the church flock, Memorial Day, the date—the day—made perfect sense. Word quickly spread that Memorial Day 1910 would be no ordinary holiday on the bluff on the west side of town. "Memorable Day!" the papers called it, in honor of the proposed church building. Elliott was pleased.

The idea to recognize the war dead with a day of commemoration can be attributed to dozens of communities that organized events adorning the gravesites of local soldiers killed in the Civil War. Even Carbondale, home of one of the earliest Illinois infantry regiments, has a stone marker that recognizes it as the first site of a Decoration Day Ceremony (although it was held several years before such a formal holiday existed). Their reasoning is valid, but others cities also claimed the distinction. Holding prayer ceremonies at gravesites and throwing flowers on graves was not an original concept, but beyond the church groups, large community turnouts of people of all faiths and races, whether churchgoers or not, were gaining momentum and support, stirred by both the size and scope of the costly war. Nearly every town in America had buried dead from the horror of the Civil War.

Columbus, Mississippi, was one town that buried many. After the bloody Battle of Shiloh, many of the wounded and war dead were sent by train to the small Southern town just above the Tombigbee River. Thousands of soldiers on both sides of the battle were interred at the hopefully named Friendship Cemetery. In April of 1866, several Columbus women went to the cemetery and placed flowers on the graves, not just upon the fallen Confederates, but Union soldiers as well. The *Mississippi Index* praised the event:

> *"We were glad to see that no distinction was made between our own dead and about forty Federal soldiers, who slept their last sleep by them. It proved the exalted, unselfish tone of the female character. Confederate and Federal—once enemies, now friends—receiving this tribute of respect."*

The act prompted Francis Miles Finch to write a poem, famously titled *The Blue and the Gray.*

> *...From the silence of sorrowful hours*
> *The desolate mourners go,*
> *Lovingly laden with flowers*
> *Alike for the friend and the foe;*
> *Under the sod and the dew,*
> *Waiting the judgement-day;*
> *Under the roses, the Blue,*
> *Under the lilies, the Gray.*

The four local women were eventually given credit for the kind gesture, and their story is remembered today in Columbus, where Memorial Day services are still carried out in the same manner.

The New York town of Waterloo, built along the banks of the Cayuga-Seneca Canal, holds the official distinction of being the "birthplace of Memorial Day," thanks to a presidential proclamation signed by Lyndon B. Johnson in 1966. The effort was originally spearheaded by the governor of New York at the time, Nelson D. Rockefeller, who recognized Waterloo as the first village-wide, annual observance of a day to honor the war dead. The local resolution was inspiring enough to be taken up by Congress, passed by the House and Senate, and sent to the President for approval. Here's Waterloo's story: 100 years earlier, in the summer of 1866, Henry Welles, a druggist, suggested a day of social gathering not only to honor the living soldiers but remember the fallen ones too. General John B. Murray supported the idea and instituted a plan. It was more like a funeral procession. Flags were flown at half-staff and black bunting was hung in respect as soldiers and towns-folk marched to three village cemeteries and placed flowers on the gravesites. The next year, in similar fashion, they did it again, and again the following year, and in each year since.

Perhaps the largest and earliest pre-Decoration Day ceremony was held in Charleston, South Carolina, in a large field known as the Race Course, where prized horses once ran. During the Civil War, the infield was used as a prisoner-of-war camp. Hundreds of mostly young men were either held there or awaited transfer to larger prison camps, like Belle Isle in Richmond or Andersonville in Georgia. Many never made it out of the Race Course, suffering from sicknesses like dysentery, which spread quickly in the inhumane conditions and tight quarters. Some 257 men perished and were quickly buried in a pasture nearby.

In May of 1865, just a year after the war ended, several Charleston residents went out to see the gravesites, just mounds of dirt really, and still fresh, noted one observer, "with the marks of the hoofs of cattle and horses and feet of men." They decided to erect a fence and place a monument on the site.

Then, on May 1, 1865, May Day, nearly 3,000 local schoolchildren

FAR LEFT: General John A. "Black Jack" Logan.

LEFT: Old Abe, the "soldier bird" of Wisconsin's Eighth Regiment.

Photographs courtesy the Library of Congress

and "double that the number of grown-ups" went to the Washington Race Course with bouquets of roses and other "sweet smelling flowers." James Redpath, known as "Uncle James," a witness, remembered the event. "The children marched from the Race Course singing the John Brown Song and then, silently and reverently, and with heads uncovered, they entered the burial ground and covered the graves with flowers.

"It was the first free May Day gathering they ever enjoyed," Redpath noted, referring to the "colored children" present and their parents, former slaves.

Three years later, on May 5, 1868, General John A. Logan of the Union Veterans—the Grand Army of the Republic—established a day for all Americans to decorate with flowers the graves of war heroes. He picked the end of May, it's believed, because that's when spring flowers would be in full bloom. On May 30 that same year, the first Decoration Day ceremony was held at Arlington Cemetery across the Potomac at the site of the Arlington Mansion, once the home of General Robert E. Lee. Bands played and General James Garfield, a future president, spoke. General Ulysses S. Grant and his wife were also there.

After Garfield's lengthy speech—which lasted nearly two hours—on a day "somewhat too warm for comfort" the *New York Times* reported, war veterans, some still limping from their battle injuries, were led by schoolchildren from the Soldiers and Sailors orphan home to the cemetery grounds, where they placed flowers on every gravesite of both Union and Confederate soldiers. It was a sign of unity in a still-fractured nation.

General Logan's declaration was likely inspired, at least initially, by a day in April 1866 near his hometown of Murphysboro, near the Illinois southern border. In Carbondale, Illinois, he was joined by 212 veterans at Woodlawn Cemetery for a community-wide observance. Logan stirred the large crowd with his inspiring words. "Every man's life belongs to his country, and no man has a right to refuse when his country calls for it," he exalted.

The General's words were held in high regard. Due to his bravery and steadfast loyalty to his men during battles, Logan was as popular a war hero in Illinois as President Grant. His presence was in demand, not only in honor, but in respect of those who sacrificed their lives. Several months after the cemetery event in Carbondale, on October 11, 1866, General Logan arrived in Peoria for the dedication of the Civil War Monument at the courthouse square. There he witnessed firsthand the lengths a city would take to honor its fallen heroes. Bands played as a grand parade of citizens and soldiers traveled down Peoria's downtown streets lined with onlookers, some hanging precariously from tree branches to get a better look. Logan, a physically imposing man, not in size, but in features, was easy to spot. Due to his slick, jet-black hair; thick, bushy mustache; and dark, focused eyes, his soldier's affectionately called him "Black Jack." General Grant called him his "best officer." Astride his horse, Logan rode alongside his marching unit. "As the procession passed along Adams Street, the space each side was filled with people loudly cheering and manifesting the greatest joy," the paper reported. "It moved down Adams Street, countermarched, and after marching about the principal streets disbanded into the square to listen to dedication exercises."

Logan and other dignitaries, including military men and politicians, were scheduled to speak, but all were upstaged briefly by a veteran bald eagle named Old Abe, the "soldier bird" of Wisconsin's Eighth Regiment, once led by General Logan. Riding a carriage, perched in front of the infantry marching companies, the majestic bird flapped its wings, and the crowds cheered their approval.

Mary Logan. Photograph courtesy the Library of Congress.

Later, at the viewing stand, when the drapery was removed and the new statute unveiled, there was a likeness of Old Abe, cast in bronze sitting atop the stone shaft, a symbol of resolve and freedom, a fitting tribute to America's war dead.

When it was Logan's turn to speak, the general did not disappoint. Evoking a dying soldier's last wishes, he passionately intoned, "Tell my wife, tell my sister, mother, that I died with my face to the enemy; that my country might live; that the principles of liberty and freedom might be enjoyed; and that they might be protected by the laws and Constitution."

Two years later, Logan's wife, Mary, visited a cemetery in Petersburg, Virginia, and was emotionally moved by what she observed. Her recollections of that day were later published:

"The weather was balmy and spring-like and as we passed through the rows of graves I noticed that many of them had been strewn with beautiful blossoms and decorated with small flags of the dead Confederacy. The sentimental idea so enwrapped me that I inspected them more closely and discovered that they were everyone the graves of soldiers who had died for the Southern cause."

Mrs. Logan suggested to her husband that the North should do the same for its fallen soldiers. "Upon our return General Logan was much interested in the account we had seen," she recalled, "and I remarked to him that I had never been touched as I was by seeing the small flags and withered flowers that laid on their graves." Logan was moved by his wife's words. She wrote, "At this General Logan said that it was a beautiful revival of the custom of the ancients in thus preserving the memory of the dead, and that he as commander-in-chief of the Grand Army of the Republic would issue an order for the decoration of the graves of Union soldiers."

Logan issued the order and made Memorial Day, then also known as Decoration Day, a national holiday. The proudest act of his career, the general would later say. In a speech commemorating the new holiday, he said, "This Memorial Day, on which we decorate their graves with the tokens of love and affection, is no idle ceremony with us, to pass away an hour; but it brings back to our minds in all their vividness the fearful conflicts of that terrible war in which they fell as victims."

THROUGH THE years, in Peoria, as in other cities of its size, Memorial Day traditions were solidly established. Marches were planned to cemetery sites; distinguished orators would raise the spirits; and ceremonies, like one traditionally held at the shore of the Illinois River, would inspire the living. "One of the admirable activities of Memorial Day is that of strewing flowers on the surface of the navigable rivers," the *Peoria Evening Star* reported. "In recognition of the services of our heroic solders who have won such laurels for our Navy, not only in the Revolution and in 1812, but in the Civil War and with Spain." A poem was recited at the site:

We give you a tender message
O fragrant and beautiful flowers
A message more felt than spoken
For the deathless heroes of ours,
A token of love we are giving
In thoughts that cannot be said
Of measureless thanks for the living
For heroic acts of the dead.

But in Peoria, on Memorial Day 1910, there was a respectful buzz throughout the city. By early light, townsfolk were arriving at the vacant corner on the West Bluff just off the city's Main Street. There would be time for solemn gravesite services later, but for now they were curious to see the start of a church-building in a single day, the one they'd read about in the paper. With hundreds watching, the hammer-wielding men lined up for the signal, and with the first strike, the work began. The crowd bellowed its approval.

Elliott keenly supervised the start of operations, but was too anxious. He grabbed a hammer and began striking away. His actions were valiant, but his aim was wildly off. "The first man to come to grief," the papers teased. Elliott had struck his thumb.

"Did he swear? Did he jump up and down and give utterance to his feelings?" the *Peoria Evening Star* asked. "No indeed! He stood up and shouted 'Hallelujah,' in a loud voice, sucked his thumb and went to work with renewed vigor."

Elliott was the perfect man to lead this charge. A railroad man by trade, he headed the Demurrage Association, which imposed fees for freight cars detained by shippers beyond their scheduled loading or unloading times. Often called "free time," such delays were costly to railroads. Elliott's job was to collect fines and diffuse angry disputes. "The shipper may be overcharged in freight several dollars," an 1887 annual report of demurrage and car efficiency reported, "but let him see an item of 'Demurrage......$1' on his freight bill and a vigorous protest is forthcoming." In essence, Elliott was a problem-solver. "You can't learn how to swim by just hanging up your clothes," he once told a group of railroad officials, concerning freight issues like costs, weights, and delays, which were all divisive topics. At the time, large railroad companies were making the rules regarding shipping times and cargo, always in their favor and usually for extra profit. Critics argued it was price gouging. But there were no rules to follow. A national push was being made to find some uniformity in car-service, and Elliott was called to supervise efforts by railroads in Illinois, Iowa, and Indiana. Oftentimes this led to contentious debates that played out in the courtrooms rather than meeting rooms. "Cars are not railroad tracks as store-house," Elliott once argued a challenge. "But as vehicles of transportation, and where consignees fail to remove lading within a reasonable time after transportation has been consummated, consignees perpetrate a wrong, which, in law and justice, they must pay for." Elliott was a man of convictions, but frank and

Church building, Memorial Day, May 30, 1910, Peoria, IL. Photograph courtesy the Peoria Historical Society Collection/Bradley University.

honest among his peers. He earned a reputation as a fair but tough negotiator. "The association, comparatively small when he became identified with it," the papers reported, "had of late years increased to large proportions."

Elliott was also a deeply religious man, often using his faith and invoking God's will—even in his work—a trait he passed along every Sunday to his Bible class at the Howard Street Christian Church. "A sterling man of character," the papers commended. So when Mr. Elliott came up with the idea for building a church in one day, besetting his reputation, it's likely there were no objections. Predicting a day's work based solely on time, nature, and man's willpower, however, was another matter. Once he had picked the date, Elliott made sure the plan stayed the course, no matter the odds.

Fearing backlash or defection, Elliott excused those who might be susceptible to conditions. "Old men will not be expected to work in rain," he announced. "Nor any man asked to do so against his will." But few were willing to walk away. And as it turned out, the weather was never a factor.

"While one gang is laying flooring another will be busy with the siding…and another will be busy with the rafters," the papers said. More than 50 carpenters showed up to "donate their day's work."

The women of the church worked as well. They served meals so the men could keep up a constant work schedule. Elliott obliged their curiosity and spirit, however, by offering each lady who wished to "a chance to drive in a nail." Many took him up on the offer.

With determination and resolve, the workers and volunteers continued their steady pace. Then the lumber ran out. Due to a miscalculation in planning, there was a shortage of materials. The men were relieved. They put down their tools and took a much-needed break. The papers noted the apparent embarrassment with grace: "In the middle of the afternoon came a lull in the hammer harmony." In quick order, more lumber was carted in and the work carried on. "If they hadn't run short of lumber, they could have cut a couple of hours off," the *Peoria Journal-Transcript* kindly opined.

Soon the walls were up, the roof was set, and the buckets of paint were ready. The frame of the 24-by-60-foot building was finally visible. The ceiling stood 12 feet high with a total building height of 25 feet. Inside was room for 300 people. There would be no benches, only chairs.

By nightfall, the work was complete except for some painting. "It stands this evening at Main and Underhill, where no church has stood before," the *Journal-Transcript* reported with unsparing praise. "It is no mighty structure of brick and stone, of marble façade or illumined windows, but it is more. It is an inspiration and an example. It is the work without which faith counts for nothing. When in the morning there had been a vacant lot on which had been constructed a brick foundation, the early evening saw a completed church edifice, walled, roofed and floored, lined and celled, wired and with fifteen electric lights installed, the exterior given its first coat of paint, a brick approach laid from the sidewalk to the front steps; the lot leveled off, a coal shed built and painted and a sign up on the front of the church edifice proclaiming it was The West Bluff Christian Chapel."

Elliott announced to the faithful that not only was the building finished, it was also free of debt. There had been a $40 shortfall in the morning, but due to donations throughout the day, that amount was wiped out. He thanked the pastor of another church, the Reverend William Price, a former bricklayer, for donating all the laid

Congregation of the West Bluff Christian Chapel gathers at the church built in a day. Photograph courtesy the Peoria Historical Society Collection/Bradley University.

bricks. Then he proudly entered the building with the others for that evening's prayers.

At sunset, the first service was held at the new church. A small organ was brought in, and through the open windows music filled the crowded streets. Inside, the weary workers bowed their heads and prayed. On this Memorial Day 1910, they had done their job. "They had blisters on their palms and splinters in other places," the papers reported, "but there was gladness in their hearts."

"Church Build in One Day!" the headline proudly proclaimed. "They did it."

The next month, in June, the church was formally dedicated.

THE STRUCTURE at Main and Underhill stood proudly for several more Memorial Days as Elliott had intended, as a place of fellowship mainly used for Bible study and Sunday school classes. Then, in 1913, as fate would have it, the building took on a more significant role. That year, in downtown Peoria, the First Christian Church was consumed by fire and destroyed. The West Bluff site was the only other place to hold services. So each Sunday, the tiny but distinguished chapel on the bluff was overflowing with parishioners, many standing outside the door just to hear the preacher speak.

Elliott would have been proud to see his idea take on such importance. It was the cultivation of his and others' efforts that the building was even available to use as a substitute for the congregation in a time of need. But he never lived to witness it. Stricken by an illness so suddenly that most Peorians never knew he was sick, Elliott passed away at home in his bed on November 10, 1910, surrounded by his wife and three children. He was 48. Less than six months after the church was built, the man who helped mastermind and construct it was gone.

"He always had a pleasant word and a smile for everyone," the papers read the next day, referring to his jovial reputation. His actions as a leader were also praised. In a lengthy tribute, Elliott was commended for his "most active" work in the community and church. His tireless efforts on Memorial Day were also mentioned. "He had much to do with the recent building of a mission on the West Bluff," the article stated. "It was his thought and his ambition to build a church in a single day's time, and accomplished that with a corps of workers." With Elliott's death, the legacy of the church suffered from the loss of its most ardent proponent. Perhaps if he had lived, he could have saved it. No one will ever know.

Here's what happened after he was gone. The fire at the downtown site was a notable absence for the congregation, so the move to the West Bluff Chapel was certainly necessary and convenient, but cramped. The building at Main and Underhill was too small to contain an expanding church community. So plans were made to build a bigger sanctuary. But it would take time. Eight years later, in 1924, a roomier church was built that sat a mile west at Kellogg and Clark Street in an area now known as West Peoria. After the new church was dedicated, it was determined the former West Bluff Chapel was no longer needed. There was no other choice. With heavy hearts, the church sold the land and building to local merchants. The West Bluff Christian Chapel sign above the door was taken down. For years, the building was sold and resold and housed several businesses which failed to ignite. Finally, time and opportunity ran out. The neighborhood's business district along Main Street was growing and more space was needed. The building eventually came down to make room for a parking lot.

Until then, on every Memorial Day, among the names of dignitaries, honored guests, speakers, and services listed in the paper
that day, there was always a symbolic mention of recognition for
the year a church was built in a single day. Elliott's thinking was
correct. Having it on a holiday secured its place in the pathos of
time, at least initially. The mentions ended, however, and also quite
symbolically, when the building was sold and eventually razed.

Like the building on Main Street, the original Civil War monument dedicated by General Logan also didn't survive. "The Shaft,"
as it was affectionately referred to by locals, was moved in 1870 to
make room for a new sidewalk at the courthouse. It sat in a different location on the square grounds until 1962 when, so weather-
beat and cracking, it was mercifully taken down. No one seemed
to care the eyesore was finally gone. By that time, a more impressive monument had been built and dedicated by President William
McKinley in October 1899. Called *Soldiers and Sailors* (although
sculptor Fritz Triebel named his piece *Defenders of the Flag),* the
68-foot-tall monument still stands majestically on the southeast
side of the square at Main and Adams Street. That would be the bottom of Main Street in downtown Peoria. Today, the busy stretch of
Main Street, which extends west of downtown on the bluff between
High Street and Western Avenue, is filled with niche restaurants,
quirky shops, business offices, a few residences, and Bradley University. The corner of Main and Underhill where the West Bluff
Chapel once stood blends in with the rest of the landscape; it's
nothing special.

There is no exact date recorded when the "church built in a single
day" eventually came down. Apparently no one fussed and no large
crowds showed up to witness the demolition. Like the old statue, a
once-proud symbol became just an aging nuisance, due to wear and
neglect, its usefulness now well past its prime. But sadly, after it's
gone, what's left is a perceptible void. Where there once stood a
structure built on faith and determination, there was now just an
empty slab. Even the local papers, so unstinting in praise when the
church went up, missed a glowing opportunity for a lasting tribute.

A chance to point out, in rich irony, that it likely took more than
a day to remove it.

STAND-UP STATESMEN

Among the least remembered—although some might say most interesting—features of Benjamin Harrison's presidency was that he was the first sitting president to ever have his voice recorded. It was around 1889, nearly 12 years after Thomas Edison invented the wax cylinder phonograph, but the first year it was mass produced. The recording is as remarkable as it is bland: "As President of the United States," Harrison begins methodically, with a slow and measured timbre, "I was present at the first Pan-American Congress in Washington, D.C. I fully believe that with God's help, our two countries shall continue to live side-by-side in peace and prosperity. Benjamin Harrison." Perhaps a meatier subject would have required more time, something Edison had yet to perfect. Regardless, in hindsight, its significance in invention alone speaks volumes. This, however, was several decades after Abraham Lincoln's death. So Lincoln was never recorded. However, interest in his speaking voice still sparks debate today. Likely, it has as much to do with the number of Lincoln impersonators as there is just plain curiosity. So historians have gone through eyewitness recounts of Lincoln's speeches to try and come up with some representation of what Lincoln may have sounded like. Twangy and high-pitched with a slight Southern drawl seems to be the most popular assessment. If true, Lincoln would have certainly turned heads when he spoke. Lincoln laughed a lot too, sometimes at his own expense, oftentimes at others'. So what did his laugh sound like? Isaac Arnold, a friend, recalls waiting outside Lincoln's White House office and hearing a "burst of mirth" coming from behind the partition. The "neigh of a wild horse on his native prairie is not more undisguised and hearty," Arnold recalled. Lincoln spent more years as a lawyer than a politician and he generally liked it. Most of his humorous anecdotes come from these years. The next story takes Lincoln, the lawyer, to Metamora, Illinois, near Peoria, for a scandalous murder trial. The tale itself, about Lincoln representing an old woman who killed her drunkard husband, is not one lost to time. Hardly anything Lincoln said or did is these days. Lincoln biographers have used the Metamora story to represent the President's penchant for humor, especially in his work as a circuit attorney. But its origins go deeper. Like the set-up before a punch line, the tale here has a backstory. It's about a deep friendship, a broad sense of humor, and how Lincoln often proved that a good joke always had a time and place. Lincoln's laugh, however it may have sounded, would have surely followed.

A MOST spirited conversation occurred in a Charleston, Illinois, hotel room in 1835 between two men, one a lawyer and the other soon to be a lawyer; who were both born in Kentucky—only a month apart—and whose last names started with the letter L. In fact, they both shared the first three letters of their last names: L-I-N. One of the men you know much more famously than the other. His name was Abraham Lincoln.

The other man was U.F. Linder.

In the annals of Illinois history not many people recognize the name Usher Ferguson Linder. Born on a small farm in Elizabethtown, Kentucky, Linder came to Illinois in the summer of 1835. By then, he was married and had two children, a son and daughter. He was an educated man, but financially broke and seeking work as an attorney. He had exhausted all his opportunities in Kentucky and was still destitute, oftentimes asking for credit to get a drink in a local tavern and oftentimes getting turned down. A change of scenery was necessary, he determined.

So the family packed up and traveled the National Road of Indiana north then west into Illinois. Linder's father lived in Terra Haute, then a part of early Illinois, which was bounded on the east by the Wabash River. The family stopped there briefly but continued to Greenup, Illinois, and eventually landed in Charleston in Coles County. It was there, barely steps into the eastern half of the new state, that Linder decided to settle his family.

Linder was impressed by the state's abundance and beauty. "It looked to me like a vast wilderness of flowers, with a soil as rich and fertile as ever a crow flew over," he wrote. The promise was in the

Coles County Courthouse in Charleston, IL, where Usher Linder lived and served. Photograph courtesy the Library of Congress.

land, Linder thought. "It seemed to me as if the Lord had created it as a paradise for farmers."

Linder could tend land, taught as a child by his father, but he foresaw a new opportunity in Illinois, a chance to pursue his career in law and give his family a stable life on the prairie. Linder's exultations of his new home, however, were short-lived. The water as he described it was "unfit even for a beast to drink." Sickness enveloped the entire town, then tragedy. Three months after displacing his family to Illinois, Linder's youngest, a boy named John, succumbed to the chills and fever. A grieving and despondent Linder resolved to escape back to his native home. "Illinois seemed to have no charms for me," he recalled in his memoirs several years later. He longed for the "hills, knolls and valleys" of Kentucky where running brooks of "purling fountains gushed in coolness from the hillside, and went dancing and babbling to the sea."

He vowed to return to his birthplace and "accept poverty as a boon."

"If we could only be blessed with health," he impassionedly wrote.

But as the sickness subsided and the family recovered, Linder had a change of heart. "I begin to look about," he recalled, and added, "to see if there was not something for me." He found acceptance and an opportunity. There was good work for an upstart attorney, he was told. Soon he began to ride the circuit. "In a country of comparative strangers," a scholar once wrote of Linder's early days as an Illinois lawyer, "Linder was very poor. But with his talent, imagination, and ready wit, he did not remain unknown for long." Linder made his mark, eventually earning a reputation as a "profound lawyer" and "brilliant orator." Known as the "Gentleman from Coles," Linder's accomplishments were lauded by his peers. A friend and fellow lawyer, Joseph Gillespie, wrote about Linder, "I never felt a defendant in a criminal case was safe from a verdict when Linder prosecuted, no matter what evidence might be in his favor."

Unlike Lincoln, a defense lawyer, Linder was prosecutor. He was also hard-headed. In one case, Linder defended, rather than prosecuted, a man. Defending clients was not his specialty, but Linder charged into the fray like an angry bull. It illustrates the man's stubbornness to win a case not on principle, but for retribution.

As the story goes, a man named Deevers, a landlord who lost an ear in a scuffle, sued an assailant for $1,000. Deevers needed a sharp lawyer like Linder, who was conveniently in town and available, the landlord was told. In a surprising twist, Linder's services were first sought by the defendant, which Linder turned down, anticipating that the landlord, Deevers, would employ him as a prosecutor, his métier. To everyone's surprise, Deevers refused and hired an acquaintance of Linder's instead. Linder was offended by the apparent snub and perhaps slightly embarrassed by it too. In anger, he responded by striking a deal with the defendant, immediately became his attorney, and vowed to give both Deevers and his unfortunate chosen lawyer "hell," in Linder's own words.

Lincoln would likely have had more self-restraint in such matters. But the law was a fickle business. Lincoln once wrote Linder during a personal crisis involving Linder's son: "We have talked about the defense of criminals before our children; about our success in defending them; have left the impression that the greater the crime, the greater the triumph of the acquittal." The impression, Lincoln implied, was misguided. Linder had every right to defend a man, however guilty he may seem, and prevail. But as Lincoln subtly suggested, perhaps teach the "criminal" a lesson in the process. This was more impressive than bragging about the win.

Linder had little time for Lincoln's moral platitudes when it came to the law. The one time he played defense lawyer, he did so because *he* felt wronged, not the other way around. In Linder's eyes, prosecuting or defending a client still required the self-effacing ability to cajole a jury—something he was very good at. Lincoln persuaded juries with his passion and thoughtful arguments. Linder was all showmanship.

In his closing remarks of the Deevers trial, Linder was masterful, Gillespie recalls. "It seemed to me that he had acquired absolute dominion over the jury and that if he had called them to render a verdict of guilty against poor Deevers, they would have done so." Knowing the case was clearly in Deevers' favor, Linder reasoned the only chance for victory was wooing the jury with his natural ability to entertain. He could charm the ladies with humor and wit, he thought. So he asked the judge to load the jury box with women. The judge, clearly intrigued by the request and perhaps unimpressed by the proceedings as a whole, granted Linder's request.

The judge's instincts, if he desired dramatic entertainment, were correct. The case suddenly became good theater. Linder took charge. He worked the room like a stage comic. "The jury, the audience, everybody was convulsed with laughter," Gillespie continued, "from the beginning to the end of Linder's argument."

Linder won the jury over by ridiculing Deevers, poking fun at the case, and chastising Deevers' own ignorance for not picking the best lawyer available when he had the chance. "He literally laughed the case out of court," Gillespie wrote.

Deevers was dumbfounded. "He looked very much like a man going to the gallows," Gillespie remembered. Deevers walked away empty-handed, later admitting he made a terrible mistake. "What a fool I was," he said, "for not hiring Linder." But this was just a "specimen case," exclaims Gillespie. Linder would use similar tactics in other cases. It became something of a trademark. "He had a soul full of humor; it beamed in his eyes and glowed in his countenance."

As his reputation grew, Linder's services were requested elsewhere, but partially due to health reasons, he stayed close to home, only accepting cases in nearby counties and avoiding the grueling circuit, where many lawyers spent as much time traveling the choking dirt roads by horseback, carriage, or foot as they did inside courtrooms arguing cases. Linder kept busy in his hometown of Charleston, a thriving Indian settlement before the Blackhawk War, where remnants of the native homesteads, abandoned after the skirmishes ended in 1832, still lined the banks of the swiftly moving streams and rivers nearby that would forever bear the names of its first inhabitants, the Wabash and the Kickapoo.

It was there in a Charleston hotel room that Linder first met Lincoln. Both men were legal-minded, and Lincoln was in town to witness a session at the courthouse. Coincidences aside, as they talked, the two men genuinely enjoyed each other's company.

"I'm in town to visit my father and stepmother," Lincoln told him. Thomas, his father, had moved to a farm just outside Charleston several years before, he explained. "But I sought more woodland to build a home, so I did not stay." Instead, the young Lincoln traveled farther west to Sangamon County and settled in an area known as New Salem.

Linder sized him up. "He was a very modest and retiring man," he would later recall, "and did not make any impression upon me, or any other member of the bar." But the two men shared an agreeable bond. Linder knew Lincoln's relatives from his boyhood in Kentucky and the conversation turned informal, even homey. Lincoln asked about his uncle, named Mordecai, or "Old Mord," as Linder remembered calling him. Linder regaled the attentive Lincoln with tales about Old Mord: "A man of considerable genius," he exclaimed, but also "a man of great drollery" who would "almost make you laugh to look at him," Linder said. Old Mord was quite the storyteller, Linder explained, "and they were generally on the smutty order," he added. One particular tale pleased Lincoln immensely. "I once heard [Old Mord] tell a bevy of fashionable girls that he knew a very large woman who had a husband so small that at night she mistook him for the baby," Linder said. "On one occasion, she armed him with a diaper and was singing to him a soothing lullaby, when he awoke and told her the baby was on the other side of the bed."

Hearty laughter must have filled the room. For Lincoln loved to laugh and this particular yarn, told quite amusingly, and originating with a blood relative, was especially pleasing, since it seemed to mirror his own folksy brand of humor. Linder's description of Old Mord as "honest, tender-hearted, and to the last degree charitable and benevolent" could have also described Lincoln.

After such a friendly and jovial exchange, the two men must have marveled at not having the good fortune of meeting each other until that day, considering how close together they were born (Lincoln was five weeks older than Linder) and in the same county of Hardin, Kentucky. But their mutual appreciation for telling a good story and enjoying a good laugh would bind them together for the rest of their lives. Lincoln always sought friendships with those who impressed him, both intellectually and humorously. Linder did both.

This leads us to Lincoln's laugh. Although it's hidden deep within the introspective spirit and sadness that highlight much of his adult life, a great deal has been written about Lincoln's ability to laugh– at himself, at others, and especially at a good joke. It is as much a fact as it is lore, especially in books about his personality, that the statesman had an uncanny ability to strike up a lively conversation and usually end it with laughter. "He was the most exquisite humorist I have ever known in my life," wrote Colonel Alexander McClure in tribute to Lincoln. "His humor was always spontaneous, and that gave a zest and elegance that the professional humorist never attains."

In person, Lincoln was a cut-up. He liked to reciprocate and delight an audience with his—or other persons'—humorous words. While he certainly enjoyed hearing a good yarn, he most enjoyed telling it. "As he neared a pith or point of the joke or story," his friend, Judge David Davis, once exclaimed, "every vestige of seriousness disappeared from his face. His little gray eyes sparkled; a smile seemed to gather up, curtain-like, the corners of his mouth; his frame quivered with suppressed excitement; and when the point—or 'nub' of the story, as he called it—came, no one's laugh was heartier than his."

Lincoln's wildly vast repertoire of jokes and tales were not his own, however, but others'. The stories he told were not original, as author Benjamin Thomas points out in his analysis of Lincoln's humor published in 1981, "although he often embellished and improved them."

Lincoln was usually absolved by his own admittance for stealing a good line. "He himself repeatedly disclaimed authorship," Thomas writes, "and described himself as merely a retail dealer." His proficiency, Thomas continues, "lay rather in a retentive memory." Lincoln's friends all agreed. "He did not forget the good things he heard," Charles Sumner once wrote about Lincoln, "and was never without a familiar story to illustrate his meaning."

Most of Lincoln's closest friends understood and appreciated his penchant for storytelling. They laughed along, even if they were the target of his playful, but often biting, jabs. Linder was the exception. During a chance meeting in a Charleston hotel room, Linder made Lincoln laugh with his jokes and tales of Lincoln's kinfolk back home. They became fast friends thanks to Lincoln's love for a good story, usually a humorous one, and Linder's ability to tell it. Lincoln would remember them all.

Thanks to Linder, years later, Lincoln would pull one out of the hat, so to speak, while covering a case in Metamora, Illinois, near Peoria.

METAMORA SITS off the east bluff of the Illinois River, about 18 miles northeast of Peoria. Settled in 1848, farmers especially liked its location, a fertile stretch of prairie land, ideal for growing stubborn crops. "High dry and gently undulating plain thus insuring perfect natural drainage," the *Metamora Sentinel* explained in 1898. Built by eastern travelers, mostly New Englanders, who first called the town Hanover, then changed it to a more Indian-sounding name, after an old chief named Metamora, the land was rich and productive not just for growers, but for everyday citizens who adorned the outside of their homes with "private gardens of beautiful flowers, delicious small fruits and vegetables." In the center of town was "the square, filled with sensory flowers, pathways and benches." Businesses surrounded the square and the townsfolk would gather in its confines to shop, converse, and hear the news of the day. When the Civil War broke out, a box was placed in front of the post office, where the postmaster would read the dispatches to an assembled crowd.

Lawyers in the state, who would stay for weeks in Metamora, the county seat of Woodford County, would argue cases in the courthouse and then step outside to converse, some say settle disputes, in the town square. "We have the most beautiful park in the state outside of Chicago," raved the *Sentinel*. "Our people are models of virtue, honesty and sobriety, anyone seeking a place for residence or business can do no better."

No question, Metamora would have been a most impressive place to visit, especially for a traveling lawyer like Lincoln.

Today, in downtown Metamora, there is a statue in front of the old courthouse. It is of a woman conservatively attired in a long pioneer dress and bonnet. She faces away from a man, considerably taller than she, who is in his trademark top coat and stove pipe hat. The woman's name is Melissa Goings. Her story is remembered not as much by what she did but what she was told. Or, more importantly, how she was told and who did the telling. The statue of the man, of course, is Abraham Lincoln, who defended the poor woman in a scandalous murder case. But there is so much more to the story.

IT ALL began April 14, 1857, when the 77-year-old Roswell Goings and his 70-year-old wife, Melissa, got into an argument "over an open window," as she described it, although why they would disagree over such a trivial matter is unclear. Unfortunately, no one else was there to witness it and poor old Mr. Goings was no longer

The Metamora, IL, Court-
house where Lincoln
heard the Goings case.
Photograph courtesy the
Metamora Courthouse
State Historic Site.

around to dispute it. He was as dead as a tree stump.

Mrs. Goings claimed that her husband grabbed and began choking her. She managed to free herself from his grip and found a
piece of stove wood on the floor. Raising it high above her head,
she swung down sharply and struck her husband on the top of the
head. Badly injured, Roswell Goings stumbled out of the house. An
acquaintance later testified that he saw the old man shortly after
he was hit. "I expect she has killed me," Goings told the man. "If I
get over it, I will have revenge." Goings never got the chance. After
suffering through four miserable days, he eventually succumbed
to his injury.

The public sentiment was clearly on the side of the poor widow.
Her dead husband was both "quarrelsome and bibulous," as one
writer put it, and testimonies showed that the couple had been
"rather disagreeable" for some time. Even the old man's roots were
shady.

Born in Virginia, the pioneer farmer came to Illinois in 1839
and bought 80 acres of prime farmland in Worth Township, then
in Tazewell County. (The land eventually would become part of
Woodford County.) Goings purchased it from a man named Jacob
Loose—whose last name would prove to be appropriate. Goings
stole the land from Loose, some would say, since the large plot
had been valued at $1,500, far more than Goings' purchase price
of $150. Then, in 1843, Goings bought more property in Woodford

County: 20 acres, this time for a down payment of one bay mare. The horse was valued at $60.

Goings may not have had many friends while alive, but as a corpse he had the law on his side. When it was time for justice, the coroner's inquest came first. Immediately, there was a snag. Goings' body was buried so quickly that the coroner never got a chance to examine it. So a judge ordered the body disinterred. Two men were hired to do the grisly deed. They dug up the corpse and carried it back to the Goings' house, "where it lay" until the coroner could take a closer look. Sure enough, it was determined that a fractured skull had done him in.

Mrs. Goings was "summoned" on a coroner's warrant to appear at a hearing and held on $1,000 bail. She claimed self-defense and hired a lawyer from Peoria named Henry Grove. Grove then called on a friend for help—a tall, lanky attorney from Springfield named Abraham Lincoln.

On October 8, the grand jury handed down an indictment that said Melissa Goings did not "have the fear of God" in her, as she claimed, but "being moved by the instigation of the Devil," desired to "kill and murder" her husband. The stick of wood, the grand jury said, was an "an instrument of death."

Judge James Harriett of Pekin was called to preside. With Grove and Lincoln beside her, Mrs. Goings responded to Judge Harriett's request that she enter a plea.

"Not guilty," was her reply.

Lincoln then requested more time.

The judge denied the motion. He granted only a short recess for attorneys to prepare for a charge of first-degree murder. First-degree murder! Lincoln was shocked by such a harsh indictment. After all, the poor woman was just defending herself against a drunkard husband. Even the family thought as much.

Still, Lincoln needed more time to prepare. That was his way. As a friend remarked, "He was slow to form his opinions, and he was deliberate." Lincoln plotted his next move. Clearly, his circumvent solutions would be tested. After nearly two decades of defending clients throughout the Eighth District Circuit Court, this case in Metamora, which would prove to be Lincoln's last in Woodford

County, would challenge his legal resolve to the end. An injurious judge, it seemed, was ready to send his client—and a woman, no less—to the gallows, without even a hint of due process. In the end, Lincoln contributed to a rather unusual resolution.

Lincoln was in his final years as a lawyer and, based upon his reputation as well as victories, he had been a fine one at that. His opinion of himself, however, was a modest one, calling his own work "adequate" and letting others judge his performance, as they did, by labeling him "honest," among other generous attributes. Good thing, because first impressions were indifferent. His physical appearance and demeanor were baffling to some. In many ways, he was something of a walking contradiction. "He was the strange friend and the friendly stranger," Carl Sandburg would later write about the uneasiness of Lincoln's approach. "So tall and so bony, with so peculiar a slouch and so easy a saunter, so sad and so haunted-looking, so quizzical and comic, as if hiding a lantern lighted and went out and that he lighted again."

Lincoln's aspirations, however, were more easily drawn. He liked law work more than any other interests at the time. One time he told a friend, "I've lost interest in politics." But that would change. Even so, Lincoln insisted that his law profession would continue after his presidency was over—a promise he never got to keep.

Entering the law profession was something Lincoln decided to do because it was steady work and he thought he might be good at it. Already experienced at manual labor and several unfulfilling jobs—like working as a store clerk and flatboat pilot, among other things—Lincoln longed to put his mind to work as well. Although only semi-educated, Lincoln was well-versed, teaching himself, with some help from his family, how to read and write.

It is possible that, as a boy, Lincoln spent a fair amount of time in contentious courtrooms watching as his father battled legal issues in Kentucky. Thomas Lincoln, a carpenter and farmer, was involved in multiple lawsuits over land claims and material contracts, and the young Lincoln accompanied his elder to the courthouse for a look.

His interest in courtrooms continued after coming to Illinois. Although just a spectator, Lincoln attended the proceedings of

Justice Bowling Green, a large and disheveled man who weighed "nearly 300 pounds" and presided over his courtroom in a baggy shirt and trousers. Green was a good storyteller and jokester, which appealed to Lincoln. They struck up a friendship, and some suggest Green was influential in mentoring Lincoln to the bar.

Lincoln spent four years studying law, longer than most students in his day, and additionally he picked up considerable firsthand knowledge, thanks to Green, who frequently called on Lincoln as a character witness and juror.

Lincoln officially became a lawyer in 1836 without taking a written or oral test. There was nothing like a bar exam today. At the time, Illinois did not require it, and Lincoln easily passed the one requirement—that the person in question possess "moral character." He swore to uphold the law in front of several state justices and was on his way.

Most newly appointed lawyers at the time were on their own to start a general legal practice. Consequently, they often ended up with cases that involved the most time and effort—the "rejects" from established attorneys, in other words. Lincoln was no different. He enjoyed the so-called "mud circuit," traveling by horseback, by coach, or even on foot from town to town, reviewing and arguing cases. Eventually, he worked with several partners—a more common practice—but continued the grueling pace of a well-traveled salesman. He became known throughout the central part of Illinois as a tough but honest man who won cases, no matter how small or insignificant the amount or purpose.

Lincoln took on all cases, simple to complex. Some cases he recognized as easily defendable by the strict letter of law, but others left room for his gift of "brevity and clarity." Complex as the law can be, Lincoln stripped it down to a matter of principle and common sense, oftentimes persuading a jury to his side by simplifying the argument.

Lincoln liked to solve cases as much as defend them, sometimes giving opposing clients a reason not to pursue a claim out of lack of evidence or to maintain a clear conscience. If Lincoln said he would not take the case, it was likely that there was no case to be made.

At the same time, Lincoln didn't shy away from a good fight. For example, when a steamboat named the *Effie Alton* rammed a newly built railroad bridge over the Mississippi River, a portion of the wooden structure burned and fell into the river. The ship sank, but fortunately no one was hurt. Lincoln defended the railroad company against claims that the bridge was an obstacle in the river and therefore responsible for sinking the ship. The bridge had been a nuisance since its conception and an effort had been made, supported by the local paper, to keep the structure out of the navigational channel. It didn't work. The bridge was built, and the backlash continued. An editor of a local newspaper held nothing back when he called the bridge "Hell's Gate," referring to its movable span—and its overall worth, in his opinion. Watching the accident unfold, locals reportedly cheered from the banks when the bridge caught fire. Even the crew of the wounded ship joined in, clapping and whistling as a portion of the span went down in flames.

As a former flatboat pilot, Lincoln could likely see the argument from both sides. But the defense needed only to prove that the bridge was no more dangerous than other hazards in the river. In fact, Lincoln explained, a pilot on the Upper Mississippi should be skilled enough to navigate through the draw without breaking a sweat. The design was not the issue, Lincoln argued. The incompetence of the pilot, however, was.

And another matter: the fire. Where did it start? And was it deliberately set? All these conflicting arguments and questions ultimately confused the jury. They deadlocked.

In the end, the railroad companies claimed victory, the bridge was rebuilt, and Lincoln became an important ally of the rail industry. Both would be served well in the years ahead.

Lincoln's reputation as a practical and reasonable man spread to his law practice. Soon, people in counties in his district were talking about the plainspoken lawyer from Springfield with the tussled hair and lanky figure. He was impractical in every other sense, they were told, from his wrinkled clothes to his nasally, high-pitched voice, but he argued cases based on sound reasoning and common-sense deduction and usually won. One example occurred in 1847, during the spring term of the Tazewell Circuit Court, a county which borders Woodford. Lincoln was counseling a man

Melissa Goings and Lincoln as depicted in statue outside the Metamora Courthouse. Sculptures by John L. McClarey. Photograph by author.

named Case who claimed he was duped by two brothers who purchased from him a "prairie team" consisting of "two or three yoke of oxen and a plow." The sale was on a promissory note for $200. According to Case, the buyers never paid up, claiming they were minors and therefore not bound by the contract. The two brothers defended their apparent bad faith in the simplest of terms: ignorance. Mr. Case should have known better, they argued.

Much to the chagrin of his client, Lincoln sympathized with the two boys. When asked if Case knew the boys were minors at the time of the purchase, Lincoln responded, "Yes, I reckon so."

Lincoln then stood up and played upon the jurors' guilt instead. George W. Miner, a witness, described his tactic: "Mr. Lincoln slowly rose to his strange, half-erect attitude and in clear, quiet accents began: 'Gentleman of the jury, are you willing to allow these boys to begin life with this shame and disgrace attached to their character? If you are, I am not.'" Lincoln then turned to the opposing counsel and chastised them for leading the boys down the path of "low villainy."

"They would never have done this," Lincoln told the jury, "had it not been for the advice of these lawyers. You have in your power to set these boys right before the world."

Lincoln had cunningly turned the jury against the very men who were defending the accusers, rather than the accused themselves. Even the two brothers were nodding in approval. Without

Abraham Lincoln likeness
depicted in statue. Sculp-
ture by John L. McClarey.
Photograph by author.

even leaving their seats, the jury ruled for payment of debt, and
the boys agreed to pay up, lest they be labeled miscreants for the
rest of their lives. "The whole argument," remarked Miner, "lasted not more than five minutes."

With that kind of ideological and practical approach, Lincoln
would have been sought out by other lawyers to bring some brevity
to a complex case. A conscientious thinker like Lincoln could benefit defendants who claimed they there were wrongfully accused or
unfairly judged. It's likely the very same reason Lincoln was called
upon to serve on the Goings murder case in Metamora.

IN THE case of Mrs. Goings, Lincoln knew he had a tough one to
crack. The people were clearly on the side of the defendant, but
there was only hearsay as a defense. The law was against poor Melissa Goings and Lincoln knew her life was on the line. A first-degree
murder conviction could mean she is hanged. Lincoln asked for
more time to prepare a defense, but the judge refused. The trial
would start immediately, the same day as the arraignment. Obvi-
ously distraught from the haste of the proceedings, Mrs. Goings
pleaded with the judge to be allowed a conference with her attorney before the juror selection began. The judge granted her request,
and Lincoln and Mrs. Goings met briefly. Then Mrs. Goings
stepped outside the courthouse and was never seen again—not in
Metamora, Woodford County, or anywhere else in Illinois.

Lincoln would jokingly admit that he gave the old woman some sage advice before she disappeared. Robert T. Cassel, a justice of the peace and acting court bailiff, who was holding Mrs. Goings on the murder charge, would later confirm Lincoln's story. As he recounted it:

"Mrs. Goings was brought into court that Lincoln might talk to her. After a while I was told by the State's Attorney to bring her up for trial, but she could not be found. I asked Lincoln about her and he said he did not know where she was. I replied, 'Confound you, Abe, have you run her off?'

"'Oh no, Bob,' replied Lincoln. 'I did not run her off.'"

When Lincoln returned to the courtroom alone, the crowd gasped and the judge called order. *Where was Mrs. Goings?* he asked Lincoln directly. To answer, Lincoln told him, "She wanted to know where to get a good drink of water, and I told her there was mighty good water in Tennessee." The courtroom roared with laughter. It was a good line and Lincoln used it effectively. The judge, however, was not amused. The defendant was nowhere to be found and therefore, he determined, the case could not continue. The jury was eventually dismissed and the courtroom emptied. Many walked out still chuckling over Lincoln's joke, something they would remember more than the trial itself, or what there was of it.

Whether Lincoln actually told Mrs. Goings what he claimed to have said before she escaped is up for debate. He likely did not. But what he did that day is obvious. Earnest East, a reporter for the *Peoria Star* who revisited the case in 1953, put it this way: "Lincoln was a practical lawyer who was willing to lean towards public sentiment when it disagreed with the strict letter of the law. In this course," East determined, "he appeared to have had the tacit approval of law enforcement officers." After all, East contends, no one chased after Mrs. Goings after she ran.

East purports that Lincoln simply enlightened the old woman, knowing the case against her was solid. She was no menace or threat to society, Lincoln reasoned. So the most practical thing to do was to advise her to slip away if she chose. So he advised her and she followed his advice. Her children likely helped.

The story could end there, without further explanation, and in

most instances, it does. Today, the retelling of the murder case in
Metamora and Lincoln's supposed advice to Melissa Goings is
found anecdotally in many books and articles about the 16TH president, to emphasize his jovial and lighthearted manner. Apparently,
Lincoln liked to tell the story over and over again because the end
result still amused him as much as it did others hearing it for the
first time. "Back when I rode the legal circuit in Illinois, I defended a woman named Melissa Goings, 70 years old," Lincoln would
begin. "They say she murdered her husband..."

The story was also fictionalized in the 2012 movie, *Lincoln*. In a
scene depicting the President awaiting word from the battlefront,
the President tells a group of soldiers huddled in a cramped telegraph room about the poor old widow from Metamora: "She wanted to know where to get a good drink of water," the actor playing
Lincoln explains, finishing up the tale, "and I told her there was
mighty good water in Tennessee." The room fills with laughter.

But in referencing the story and specifically the joke, Lincoln
always gets full credit. No one mentions the other lawyer from Illinois, Lincoln's friend and colleague, Usher Linder.

But it was, after all, Linder's line.

A diary entry by Lincoln's future secretary and longtime friend
John Hay confirms it. While it may have been Lincoln's idea to free
the poor woman from the restraints of the law, Hay explains, the
story he used to diffuse his actions came from his old friend Linder.
Hay wrote, "[Lincoln] told one devilish story about Linder (a lawyer) getting a fellow off who had stolen a hog by advising him to
go get a drink and suggesting the water was better in Tennessee."

Linder probably had no idea Lincoln even used the line.

IN COLES County, Linder continued to practice law and served in
the state legislature with Lincoln and Stephen Douglas, oftentimes
feverishly debating issues with Lincoln on the House floor. Linder
had split from the Whig party, supported the Democrat Douglas,
and eventually opposed Lincoln's run for the presidency. But the
two men often greeted each other cordially, like old pals, before
Lincoln's debates with Douglas.

Despite their political differences, Lincoln always had great

Abraham Lincoln and Usher F. Linder (arms folded) from the painting of the Lincoln-Douglas Debate in Charleston, IL, by Robert Root, that hangs in the Governor's Office of the Illinois State Capitol. Print courtesy the Illinois State Capitol.

respect for Linder as a lawyer. In a speech, Lincoln said about his friend, jokingly, "In one faculty, at least, there can be no dispute of the gentleman's superiority over me, and most other men; and that is, the faculty of entangling a subject, so that neither himself, nor any other man, can find head or tail to it." Linder likely got a good laugh from it.

Before politics consumed them, as lawyers, Lincoln and Linder served several cases together, including one considered to be Lincoln's "strangest," known as the Matson slavery case when Linder asked Lincoln as a favor to defend a slave owner who moved to the North and fought to keep his slaves.

When Lincoln became president, the two men continued to correspond through letters. Although politics split them, their love for a good story, usually a funny one, was something they continued to share. Lincoln appreciated Linder's Southern-style humor and was forever grateful for the candid stories of his kinfolk back in Kentucky; Linder, in return, was quick to defend Lincoln's loose and backwoods style. Once, when another lawyer suggested to Linder that Lincoln was "wasting time" telling stories in front of juries, Linder shot back, "Don't lay that flattering unction to your soul. Lincoln is like Tansey's horse, he 'breaks to win.'"

After the Goings trial was suspended, Lincoln returned to his offices in Springfield. In the weeks that followed, legal proceedings continued, despite Melissa Goings' absence. Goings' own son, Joseph, was accused of trying to bribe a justice "ten dollars" to strike down the murder charge. He skipped town just like his mother. Lincoln returned to the Metamora courthouse to settle the case. He represented the woman's bondsmen, which included a relative, Armstrong Goings, and another man named Beck. Both were asked to defend the woman's actions in court, *scire facias*. Lincoln argued in favor of confession and avoidance, and the charges were dismissed.

Years later, Mrs. Goings was spotted in California. Not much else is known or documented about her life after escaping into the wilderness.

Lincoln was destined for the White House.

When Lincoln became President, Linder lobbied for a cabinet post in his friend's administration. He sent several letters to Lincoln explaining why he was the best choice, but he was never asked to serve. Instead, Lincoln trusted him to take care of his legal affairs in Illinois.

In April of 1865, Linder addressed his friend again. This time, it was to say goodbye. When Lincoln's funeral train stopped in Chicago on its way to its final destination of Springfield, Linder was asked to give a eulogy. Linder was despondent. He spoke in a low tone and, with deep emotion, recalled their long friendship together. "References to the many kindnesses that he had received from the President abounded in pathos and wistfulness," wrote one observer of the speech. Linder said he had hoped to personally thank Lincoln for a favor the President granted his family during the war, but never got the chance.

It was in December of 1863, while the war raged in battlefields across the South, that Lincoln stood before Congress and issued a proclamation that any enemy officer would be pardoned if he would swear, without coercion, his allegiance to the Union. It was a bold and compassionate move by Lincoln not to punish those who were thrown into a war which in some instances pitted brother against brother. Known as the Proclamation of Amnesty and Reconstruction, it provided a general pardon to either captured or deserted Rebel soldiers or Union deserters who abandoned the cause.

Several weeks after Lincoln issued the order, he received a letter. It was from his friend Usher Linder. The letter was different from others Lincoln had received from Linder, mostly frustrating rants about strategies and stark differences in handling the war.

In it, Linder told Lincoln about his son, Daniel, who had returned to Kentucky and was commissioned to serve in the Confederacy. He was captured and currently held in a Maryland prison, called Pointe Lookout. Lincoln knew Daniel well. Years before, the boy had shot a man named Ben Boyle during a heated quarrel. The victim's family cried murder. Linder would have defended his own son, but suffered from a severe bout of rheumatism and could barely move. As a concerned father and lawyer, he felt hopeless. Lincoln heard about the charges against Daniel and sent Linder a letter. "I know how you feel, Linder," Lincoln wrote, "and I can understand your anger as a father, added to all the other sentiments." Lincoln agreed to represent the boy and Linder was moved to tears by the gesture. In the end, Lincoln had little to do. The case ended up in Marshall County and the murder charges were eventually dropped when the victim survived.

Now Linder was asking Lincoln, as a concerned father, for another special request.

Lincoln responded in a letter to the Military Commander at Pointe Lookout. "If you have a prisoner by the name of Linder," he wrote, "Daniel Linder, I think, and certainly the son of U.F. Linder, of Illinois—please send him to me by an officer." Within days, the prisoner Daniel Linder stood before Lincoln in the White House. He came accompanied by a guard and a letter from Brigadier General Gilman Marston acknowledging Lincoln's request. It was a short meeting. Perhaps Lincoln only wanted to tell Daniel what a fine gentleman his father is and how proud he must be of his son, regardless of what side he chose to fight on. Lincoln turned the letter over and wrote these words: "Daniel W. Linder, the Daniel Linder named within, is the son of my friend U.F. Linder, at Chicago, Ills. Please administer the oath of allegiance to him, and send him to his father." The Attorney General at the time, Edward Bates, would later write in his diary that Lincoln wanted to release Linder in order "to gratify Linder, the father, who is an old friend."

Lincoln addressed a letter to Linder personally. Showing his penchant for using humor to lighten a serious matter, Lincoln wrote: "I'm sending your boy to you today as a Christmas present. Keep him at home."

Linder was forever grateful.

A PLOTTER'S TALE

Willebrord Snellius, a Dutch astronomer and mathematician, had a brilliant but conflicted mind. He had numbers in his head, lots of numbers. Some numbers fit together precisely and others did not. He taught theories in universities based on these numbers and drove himself completely mad trying to explain why certain numbers relate and others don't. He used a triangle and its right angle relationship to explain these theories to his students. For the ones he couldn't explain, he sought answers. He was, in essence, the 17TH century's version of *The Big Bang Theory*'s Sheldon Cooper—only as smart in his own mind as the next complex problem he solves before anyone else. Lucky for us, Willebrord Snellius was a real person. He became obsessed with measuring the meridian, used a method called triangulation—which he didn't invent, but perfected—and gave birth to modern-day land surveying. He also had 18 children. Today, Snellius' theory of triangulation is still being used by surveyors to measure land and the distance between two points of land. In America, in the mid-19TH century, when towns were being formed on prairie plots that Indians had abandoned or were forced to abandon, being a surveyor meant good work. This takes us to the origins of the city of Peoria, which have been well-researched and documented by others. That's not what this next tale is wholly about. It's about a man who came to town to plot the land, set paths, and establish boundaries. It's also about a persistent journalist who, like Willebrord Snellius, kept digging until he found the answer. Thanks to good research and writings, we have an old story to tell about an Indian, a crime, a trial, and a first for Peoria: drama in the courtroom. Like numbers in a math problem, the sums of the parts all make sense in the end.

IN 1912, as a contributing writer for the *Illinois State Journal of the Illinois State Historical Society,* a man named Bill Moon wrote an article titled "The Story of No-Ma-Que," describing a true tale about a Potawatomi Indian named Nomaque who, in 1825, came to Peoria a loner, befriended a man who lived along the river, was accused of killing another man in a drunken brawl, and ended up as Peoria County's first recorded murder suspect. Moon was not the first to tell the tale but, perhaps motivated by differing descriptions of the story, like any good researcher, he checked the books and discovered the nearly 90-year-old case at the time, "as set out in the musty records of the circuit court." It was the very first recording of the court for such matters like a trial and, as Moon notes, perhaps surprisingly, the papers were "still on file."

Nomaque was a hunter, "tall in stature and muscular," Moon writes, who, during the early part of the summer in 1825, was told by other Indians that "there was plenty of fur to be had" in *Opa*, or Wesley City, on the eastern banks of the Illinois River near a settlement known as Peoria. The white man, they explained to the curious Indian, had set up a fur company near a burned-out fort. Here Nomaque could hunt and sell his wares.

Nomaque set out alone. He traveled weeks through deep forest and thick prairie brush, each day wrapping his buckskin tighter around his shoulders as the September moon sat low and the fall chill set in. A rifle slung over his back would be used for protection against predators, but so far the trip had seen no danger. Then he heard the sound of rushing water through the thick brush. Nomaque had reached the banks of the Illinois River. In front of him, "the shining stream like polished silver, stretched away to an unexplored north," Moon writes. "To his back rose hills covered with forest."

Nomaque was pleased he had made it, but weary from the trip. "His tread was slow and measured like the movements of a clock," Moon writes about the Indian's arrival in Peoria, "his feet falling noiselessly on the sand. His head drooped as if he were tired." He set a pack down beside his feet, rested, and looked around. This was native territory to its core. In the 1820s, the settlement called Peoria was just a parcel of land, yet to be mapped. Most of its inhabitants were traders, hunters, or fishermen who set up posts to do business with the friendly Indians in the region. Nomaque felt like a stranger. "His eyes traveled across the river, and he looked wistfully at a small cluster of log cabins," Moon writes, "the homes of white men and the ruins of a log fort on the opposite bank, west and north of him."

Nomaque ended his brief respite and set out for the other side. He grabbed his pack and stepped into the chilly waters. He lopped through the ripples, watching his feet take each careful step. Thankfully, the mud-colored river was not deep. Then, startled by the sound of water churning, he looked up. A man in a canoe was headed toward him. *A white man!*

John Agee was the man's name. Agee had a trading post on the Peoria side of the river and spotted the wayward Indian struggling to cross. "Suddenly the attention of the Indian was arrested by the sound of the canoe paddle," writes Moon. "The hunter, when he saw the red man, changed his course and shot his canoe toward the place where the Indian was standing." Agee introduced himself, and Nomaque was surprised and "delighted" to hear the stranger speak his native tongue. "I have a squaw wife," Agee told the startled Indian, and invited Nomaque to his cabin. Nomaque explained that he had traveled "long and hard" and wanted to settle in the region, but for now just "intended to locate there for the winter." Agee introduced the Indian to his family and they all kindly shared an evening meal. "He felt welcome in the humble cabin with his new-found friends," Moon contends. But his welcome did not last. What happened next seems to contradict Moon's first description of Nomaque's visit, of a man who traveled far, befriended a local, and seemed genuinely pleased by the hospitality. As Moon describes subsequent events, "[Nomaque] little dreamed that a few weeks later he would be tried for murder in the same room and cabin."

Nomaque, as it turned out, spent just enough time in Peoria to earn a dubious reputation. Agee had no problem relating to the Indian; he spoke his language. But most of the townsfolk thought Nomaque was bad news from the start: a drunk, a lout, and a good-for-nothing troublemaker. Now he had killed another man without consequence or regret. The punishment was simple. Without due process of law, the hapless suspect would hang from the nearest tree. Revenge and vigilante justice would be served. That was the pioneer way. But times had changed.

The newly established Peoria County was now a judicial district and one of five regional circuit courts in the state. A judge was assigned on November 14, 1825, and on that day the legal process in the county was established. A month earlier, on October 14, outside a saloon, a white man was found dead from a stab wound. Witnesses came forward. The Indian did it, they said, the new one in town, the one who went by the name of Nomaque. Peoria County not only had its first case, but it was a murder case. A trial would be held, but where? No courthouse had as yet been built. John Agee's cabin along the river would have to do. The trial was set to begin, but one question remained.

Who would represent the accused?

JUST A year before, on June 28, 1824, four men and nearly 700 head of cattle reached the grounds of Fort Howard on the banks of Wisconsin's lower Fox River. More like a compound than a fort, Fort Howard's soldiers milling about the range of barracks nestled inside the 30-foot-high stockade of timber walls must have been alarmed by such a large faction appearing through the thick grove of trees. Hearing the rustling at first, which sounded like a rolling thunder between the tall, shadowed stalks, they raised their rifles in defense. But this was no enemy.

Major Whistler, who commanded the fort, was stunned. If he'd harbored doubts that the leader of this expedition, a man named William Hamilton, would make it safely from the prairies of Illinois, traveling some 350 miles through uncharted dense wilderness and avoiding hostile Indian tribes, then the scene before him was remarkable, if not shocking. Not only was the herd intact, save for one, but the pioneer trekkers had arrived unscathed, untouched, and—perhaps even more impressively—a week earlier than expected.

Fort Howard was a territorial post, like several in the Great Lakes region, designed to guard the newly claimed American soil against Northwest Indians. A fort site since the late 1600s, it was built by the French, then occupied by the British, who abandoned it in 1763. Americans reclaimed the land after the War of 1812.

Before establishing a fortified post, early French explorers arriving by boat were appalled and sickened by the foul stench coming from the massed algae that bloomed during the summer months. They dubbed the territory the *Bate des Puans,* which means the Bay of Bad Odors or Bay of Stinkards, before an English translation emerged that somehow disregarded the offensive for the more sublime. With the emphasis on the striking color rather than the odor, the area became more commonly known as Green Bay.

The French settlers who stayed behind held a strong British allegiance (they helped stock and feed the soldiers during the conflict), but when the war ended, they were understandably on guard. The Americans would come with a vengeance, they were told. They arrived in 1816. Four high-sailed schooners made their way up the Fox River, packed with 500 American soldiers on board.

The standoff was tense at first, until the settlers strained their eyes and recognized that the man piloting the largest of the American ships was one of their own. Augustus Grignon, a grandson of the founder of the settlement, had gone to Mackinaw a few weeks earlier to ship furs. Now he was back, this time pressed into service by the Americans who wanted nothing more than to rebuild the fort and protect the important trade route between the Great Lakes and the Mississippi. The locals were irrelevant as long as they didn't start the shooting first. It turned out that no one wished for any more bloodshed.

In time, the garrison would serve the community as a trading post, a hospital, and even host large banquets and balls. A schoolhouse was built on the grounds, complete with "books, stationary and furniture," and French settlers mingled happily with the young American soldiers whose only threats, it seemed, were fighting off the doldrums during slow months, and—during the winter—frostbite. The Indians were mostly friendly.

In 1824, under Major William Whistler's command, supplies were running low. What the fort needed was livestock to fortify the rations. But getting a herd of cattle to such a remote location, hundreds of miles north of the grassy plains and through dense forests was a seemingly impossible task. Whistler put out a call for anyone brave enough or crazy enough to try it. Twenty-eight-year-old William Hamilton, a surveyor in Springfield, Illinois, at the time, took up the challenge. Hamilton certainly wasn't crazy, but

Alexander Hamilton, father of William S. Hamilton. Photograph courtesy the Library of Congress.

he was ambitious and impulsive "When young Hamilton became obsessed with a desire he would drop everything else to appease it," author Sylvan J. Muldoon wrote in 1930. Hamilton signed a contract with the government, rounded up a posse, and informed local ranchers that he needed stock—$10 or less a head if they could spare it. Many complied. Soon, a drove of cattle awaited him on the southern banks of the Mackinaw River at Dillon's Settlement, now Dillon Township near present-day Tremont.

William Stephen Hamilton, whom his friends called "Billy," was the sixth of eight siblings, five of them boys, who grew up in a household managed mostly by their mother. Billy was the wild child, often erratic, unpredictable and adventurous, while his brothers and sisters were more passive and reserved, like their parents. William picked up on studies easily and in this manner mirrored his father, an intellectual and forward-thinker, qualities William would try to emulate as a young man.

No one could fault William from trying to follow in his father's footsteps. After all, Alexander Hamilton was an important and estimable figure. A protégé of George Washington's, a major general, signer of the Constitution, the first Secretary of the Treasury, writer of the tax laws, and, as Hamilton's biographer Ron Chernow put it, "the most important person in America never to become president."

He was also dead by the time Billy reached the age of seven.

Much like the rest of the Founding Fathers' legacies, Alexander Hamilton's reputation is cemented in platitudes today, but after his untimely death in 1804, and much to his widow's dismay, the major general's career was tarnished by political enemies who slandered the man with lies and rumors. Hamilton never got the chance to debate his critics or write a lasting memoir like his colleagues. Only letters, state papers, and essays remain to paint a picture of a complex man, loved by some and despised by others, who never compromised his principles. He is an important, often misunderstood, but revered figure in American history today. At the time of his death, however, Hamilton was a wily politician and lawyer who was deflecting barbs about a shocking illicit affair, which he did not deny, and settling old debts.

In short, being the son of the late Alexander Hamilton may not have had the same social impact or importance then that it would have in the public conscience, say, 200 years later. In fact, William, who was blessed with all the distinctively handsome features of his father, likely turned no heads, or caused any whispered chatter, in the pre-photograph era. He was a "spitting image" only to those who knew the major general personally. Although he deeply admired his parents, especially his caring mother, even as a boy, William witnessed the worst of his strict but loving father's indiscretions. Alexander Hamilton's death was the direct result of a bitter personal rivalry and rather trite political spat.

Holding a grudge over a campaign accusation, Aaron Burr, a law-

The Burr and Hamilton duel, 1804. Print courtesy the Library of Congress.

yer, politician, and all-around blowhard, challenged his old nemesis to a duel. As the story goes, Hamilton fired the first shot, but aimed errantly on purpose. Burr was left to unleash the deciding shot. "He must have assumed that, once he fired," Chernow speculated, "Burr would be too proud or too protective of his own political self-interest to try to kill him." Burr was neither. Many duels ended in draws with both parties walking away to perhaps settle another day—or another way. In this case, Burr was a more accurate shot. When the smoke cleared, Hamilton was the one lying on the ground. A friend of Hamilton's and a witness, William Van Ness, wrote, "The pistols were discharged within a few seconds of each other and the fire of Col. Burr took effect; Genl Hamilton almost fell instantly." Hamilton's bullet whizzed by Burr's shoulder and hit a tree, while Burr's shot struck Hamilton in the hip, with the ball then fracturing a rib, ripping through the liver, splintering the second lumbar vertebra, and coming to rest in the spine. The major general died a few days later.

As a teenager, William insisted on possession of his late father's private library and immersed himself in books, mostly law books. In 1815, at age 16, he went to West Point Academy, just as his military-minded father had hoped for all his boys, but William left after only a year. Many of the school records before 1838 were burned in a fire, so not much is known of Hamilton's short stint there as a student. In March of 1816, the Muster Rolls of Cadets lists William

Stephen Hamilton as "not returned from last vacation." The same was written for rolls in April, May, June, and July. In August, his name was crossed out with pencil. William never returned to West Point. Instead, he went exploring. "If his [father] had known that his son would not tolerate the military aristocracy of the Academy," one author surmised, "he would have turned over in his grave."

The young man plodded west, or as far as the Mississippi River at the time, and found work as a surveyor in Arkansas, Missouri, and Illinois. The work was arduous but rewarding. An account on the early days of landscaping summed up a surveyor's job this way: "For several months the staff waded through the unfamiliar country, making calculations, marking and laying out towns, settling boundary disputes and all those peculiar duties accompanying their profession." The general surveyor, a man named Rector, was so impressed by Hamilton's "aptitude in mapping out unsettled lands," he appointed him deputy general surveyor of the region—quite an honor for someone who hadn't yet turned 20.

For a time, Hamilton lived in St. Louis, a port area already benefiting from the region's growth. It was in St. Louis where the "youthful" Hamilton faced his most daunting challenge yet: coming face-to-face with the man who killed his father. Aaron Burr was visiting the river city and possibly plotting an "ingenious scheme." As the story goes, the young Hamilton challenged Burr to a duel to avenge his father's death, but the scowling Burr refused on the grounds of their age disparity. Hamilton, according to biographer Muldoon, "was thus compelled to permit his father's murderer to go unpunished." A nephew, Edgar Hamilton, challenges the story, claiming the two likely met, but in respect to the idea that Hamilton sought a duel: "I will say that his mother took pledges from all of her sons according to the best family traditions against dueling."

Elizabeth Schuyler Hamilton, the poor widow, had lost not only a husband but also her oldest son to a dueler's bullet. Philip Hamilton's death came before his father's but in an eerily similar manner: a first shot goes errant while the return volley hits the mark. In fact, the elder Hamilton, it is said, may have told his son to waste his first shot in honor, perhaps foreshadowing his own fate. "No," claims the nephew, in regard to the St. Louis duel story, "William S.

Hamilton loved his mother too dearly to violate a promise."

Regardless, "Billy" went on his way.

As settlers arrived and villages emerged, Hamilton plotted and charted. Soon, everyone was asking for his services. He spent time working in Springfield before traveling north, up the Illinois River, to a large piece of land carved out of a tree-studded bluff and a sandy plateau. There he would chart an area known as Peoria. It's also the first time he would put his lawyer skills to the test, as a defense attorney in a historic trial: the county's first, involving an Indian accused of murdering a white man.

The Indian's name was Nomaque.

HAMILTON ACCEPTED the challenge without question, just like he had a year earlier when he led an expedition with a herd of livestock north to save a remote outpost in the Wisconsin forest. It illustrates Hamilton's persistence and determination to overcome adversity despite the odds, a stubbornness that would later serve him well in a courtroom.

When Hamilton arrived at the banks of the Mackinaw River in Dillon's Settlement, the starting point of the long trek northward to Green Bay, he noticed something unusual. The herd of cattle had already been driven across the swollen river. This wasn't such a bad thing in his mind. The men he hired had done the deed. But instead of gloating about their accomplishment, Hamilton found them discouraged and withdrawn. One man had drowned, he was told. Hamilton chastised the men for being careless and told them the real battle and strength lay ahead in the unknown wilderness. With that, the four men and 700 head of cattle were off.

The journey was unremarkable, considering the risks involved. Hamilton followed the Mackinaw to the Fox River, then the Illinois River, oftentimes clearing trees and brush to get the cattle through. They stopped briefly at Fort Dearborn and crossed the Chicago River, then followed the shore of Lake Michigan, passing only Indian tribes north of Chicago until they reached a remote trading post just south of the Milwaukee River. A man named Kinzie, who manned the post, was on the verge of starvation. Hamilton gladly shared his provisions.

Pressing on, they reached Manitowoc and met a party of fishermen in a mackinaw boat who directed the party away from the lake and into the thick brush. They arrived at Fort Howard on June 28. According to the government contract, they were scheduled to be there on the Fourth of July. Major Whistler was pleased they arrived early, in one piece and unharmed.

To everyone's amazement, when the herd was counted, only one head was missing. Hamilton said he must have lost the cow in one of the rivers they crossed. (Later, Hamilton found out the truth. A man who assisted the crew across the Chicago River had drowned the cow on purpose, as food was scarce. He would have asked to buy it, the man claimed, but knew Hamilton would not sell a single steer, being it was government property and not his own.) Whistler was impressed. "It must be considered a matter of much luck," Muldoon wrote, "that Hamilton did not meet with one or more of the bands of mischievous savages on his way to Green Bay. There loomed the threat of cattle being stolen or worse yet a stampede, but amazingly neither occurred." After several days of rest, Hamilton took an inland route back, meeting friendly natives along the way. Following an old Indian trail south, he returned to Springfield.

The next year, he went to Peoria.

PEORIA WAS a sight to behold, nestled along the western banks of the Illinois River. At its widest point, known as Lake Peoria– described in detail in 1880's *A History of Peoria County* as "a great silver mirror, upon whose surface the sunbeams dance in joyous glee"– were many miles of fertile valley. So inspiring was the view that the first white men to come upon it–Father Jacques Marquette, Louis Joliet, and Robert de LaSalle–arriving by boat, all sought to explore the inviting vistas.

Marquette was the first. The French Jesuit priest turned explorer was told about a "Great River" with an endless path south. If true, an important trade route could be established. In 1673, along with Louis Joliet, he led an expedition that followed the Mississippi River to the mouth of the Arkansas River where, fearing reprisals from local Indians, they turned back, satisfied they had found a pathway to the open waters, a direct route to the Gulf of Mexico, but some 400 miles short of their goal. During the trip on the Mississippi, Marquette's crew noticed a pathway with footprints and followed it inland, finding a tribe of Indians he took to name the Peorias. "Having reached us at last," he wrote in his journals, "they stopped to consider us attentively." The Indians lifted their peace pipes to the sun and offered them to Marquette's men. "I now took courage," Marquette noted, "seeing these ceremonies, which are used by them only with friends, and still more on seeing them covered with stuffs, which made me to judge them to be allies."

Marquette's assumption was correct. The Peorias were friendly and accommodating, and the crew stayed several days. Marquette promised to return in "four moons," but never made it back. On the return trip, the crew was told another river branched from the Mississippi, allowing a shorter route to the Great Lakes. Exploring the Illinois River for the first time, Marquette noticed a familiar tribe's village on its banks, directly in a map line across from where he stopped on the Mississippi. The Peorias on this river were just as welcoming, and Marquette preached to the tribe.

Robert de LaSalle was more a scientist than a preacher. He ventured into the village four years later to a vastly different result. Initially welcomed by the hospitable natives, LaSalle's intentions were not as defined as Marquette's, and eventually his men grew restless and contentious with the tribe and each other. Fearing trouble, LaSalle built a makeshift fort, as he had in many locations along the Great Lakes basin, at the base of the future Peoria bluff, which served mainly as an outpost for explorers that followed.

In 1778, the French settlers came and built the first residences, hovels really, along the banks. Used mostly as a labor camp for fishermen and hunters, the land was never laid out and abandoned several times. Then, in 1813, during the war with England, an American expedition of soldiers defeated the Indians (who were considered allied with the British) and claimed the land. Believing the French were in cahoots with the enemy as well, they burned the village and built a sturdier structure, called Fort Clark.

In 1818, the fort was evacuated and subsequently burnt to the ground by the Indians. None of the early occupants of the village remained. Then, according to *A History of Peoria County,* in 1819,

Father Jacques Marquette and Louis Joliet in a canoe, with two other men, first explored the Illinois River, 1673. Painting by Edgar S. Cameron. Print courtesy the Library of Congress.

a group of aspiring men, mainly from the east, came to the Illinois River to catch and pack fish. They settled by the site of the ashes from the burned-out fort and built up. The next winter, more men came, this time with their families—and traders. In 1822, a Massachusetts furrier established the first Indian trading post.

By 1825, the population grew to just over 1,200, and the town of Peoria, now part of the newly organized Peoria County, took shape. This is when William Hamilton was summoned to survey, plot, and map the land. It's also around the same time Nomaque came to town. The two would formally meet in a makeshift courtroom.

NOMAQUE'S PREDICAMENT was hopeless. He had no defense, spoke no English, and had only one friend, it seemed: John Agee, the hunter and trader who invited the stranger into his log cabin after discovering Nomaque desperately trying to traverse the river. Agee also spoke Nomaque's language.

Not much is known about the crime itself or the motive, only accusations. Pierre (or Peter) Laundri's death was the result of a stab wound to the abdomen; that was indisputable. The weapon, witnesses claimed, was a scalping knife. Nomaque, the Indian, did it, went the consensus. Both men were drunk, but Nomaque, they said, was the instigator. In fact, it was Nomaque's newfound friend Agee who eventually turned him in. Under oath, Agee swore to the justice of the peace that he "had good reason to suspect and does verily believe that Nomaque, an Indian of the Potawatomie nation of Indians, did on the second day of October instant, stab and kill Peter Laundri." Whether he elaborated on the reasons for this act is not known.

Without a formal courthouse in the new territory, the trial would be held in John Agee's log cabin by the river. Agee would serve as translator and Hamilton—asking only for two lots as payment— would serve as Nomaque's counsel.

The Indian had few rights in the public conscience and the towns- people, who would be called as potential jurors, already pegged him a guilty man. The proceedings, however, got off to a rousing start. "Whiskey flowed freely, and at the opening session of court a visitor would have thought the event was in celebration of a holiday or a gala day," Bill Moon wrote in the *Illinois State Journal*. Despite the revelry, there was some semblance of order. The newly appoint- ed judge of the first circuit, John York Sawyer, presided over the trial. But evenhandedness would be difficult with little resource. Even within the context of the law, Nomaque was doomed.

The indictment against him was grossly slanted, almost comical in its wording, stating the Indian was likely possessed by the devil and "did not have the fear of God in him." Nomaque struck the Frenchman not just with any knife, the indictment claimed, but a "'scalping' knife," by which "Londri died."

Fearing the biased judgments toward Nomaque were tenuous at best and non-defensible at worst, Hamilton set out to convince the judge how polluted such a trial would be. He started with the jury, arguing just cause for nearly each one to be removed. One gentleman, Hamilton claimed, wasn't even a "taxable inhabitable" of the county. The stubborn judge refused each argument. Other legal wranglings on Hamilton's part also fell on deaf ears. The trial began and ended quickly.

In November of 1825, Nomaque was found "guilty" of murder and sentenced to hang. But Hamilton's job as a defense attorney, while understated to that point, began after Nomaque's hasty conviction. Now the crafty lawyer had more leeway to target certain members of the jury and their tainted verdict. One man, Hamilton argued, called Nomaque a "rascal" and appeared to have "a deep resentment against Indians as a whole." He said these incriminating words, Hamilton stated, "even before his being sworn in as a juror." Clearly this was grounds for a mistrial. The judge rejected it. A frustrated Hamilton had no other choice. He filed a motion for appeal.

In the meantime, the judge ordered Nomaque to a safe place or "place of safe keeping until the third Saturday in the month of January next between the hours of twelve and three." At that time, he proclaimed, Nomaque would be taken to "a convenient place of execution" and "hanged by the neck until he is dead." Now the only thing that stood between the convicted Indian and a date with the noose was Hamilton's skills as a lawyer.

Hamilton kept working. He appealed the case to the Supreme Court of Illinois, again a first for Peoria County, and was granted a retrial. Nomaque's life was spared this time, but a second trial would shape up to be similar to the first. Hamilton needed a new strategy. He asked and was granted time to prepare a defense. While waiting, Nomaque was held under guard by townsfolk who were paid from $10 to $15 for their service. One impromptu jailer, a man named Allen, held Nomaque at his house at the request of the sheriff. John Hamlin, a juror, described what happened next: "One night about a dozen drunken Indians met to rescue [Nomaque] and attempted to enter the door for that purpose. Allen sprang out of the back window, grabbed a clap board and rushed around the front of the house and laid about them with great fury."

"Stop, white man, stop," the Indians begged before crawling off.

Nomaque was indicted for the second time in October 1826. This time, Hamilton went back to his father's law books. He tried a different tact: to dismiss the case altogether on the grounds that the Indian was not bound by laws of the State of Illinois because his tribe had never consented that one of its members should be tried for any offense committed on Indian land by any tribunal of the state or United States. Hamilton moved that the charges be dropped, and counsel for the state demurred. The case would go back to the Supreme Court.

The delay gave Nomaque, who while under watch was "allowed to roam," a chance to escape, which he did.

In May of 1828, the case was stricken *nolle prosequi,* meaning the charges could not be proven by either the evidence or a flaw in the prosecution's case. Therefore, Nomaque, who was nowhere to be found, was a free man by law, and Hamilton, his lawyer, had prevailed.

IN 1827, Hamilton left Peoria and life as a lawyer, surveyor, and politician (he served as state legislator in a seat that would eventually be filled by Abraham Lincoln) and ventured northwest in search of more adventures and riches. Prosperous lead-ore mines were opening near the southern border of Wisconsin, just north of Galena, Illinois, and good men who enjoyed a self-reliant lifestyle and hard work were being rewarded. Hamilton built a double log home along a creek bank and struck it rich. By 1930, Billy and his miners excavated enough minerals to process 25,000 "lead pigs," or bricks of ore that weighed up to 55 pounds each.

It's also here in an area now known as Hamilton's Diggings where we get a better picture of the man. Theodore Rodolf, who worked with Hamilton, said he was a "rough and ready miner," but "cultured."

"He spoke French and his cabin shelves were filled with books, but he lived humbly," praised Rodolf, and then added without apology, "Socially he was pleasant, but not communicative, and left the impression of a rather cold distant man. He never married."

This was around the time of the Black Hawk War, where Hamilton was commissioned as a colonel in the militia, satisfying at least briefly—and likely without hesitation—his father's insistence to serve in the military. Hamilton's older brothers also honored their father's wishes by serving in the war, each in high regard and stature. But after the war ended, Billy's adventures were about to take a decisively different turn.

The Gold Rush was on and, aroused by the prospects of venturing west in search of more adventure and profits, Hamilton sold his lots in Wisconsin and left the Diggings. Despite pleas from his workers to stay, Hamilton wished them well and promised to claim his share of gold and return in two years.

Hamilton likely followed other rugged pioneers on the dangerous Overland Trail, using ox carts across barren land and private

LEFT: William S. Hamilton. Reprinted in *Alexander Hamilton's Pioneer's Son* by Sylvan Muldoon (Aurand Press, 1930). Photograph courtesy the Local History and Genealogy Collection, Peoria Public Library, Peoria, IL.

TOP: Hamilton's monument in Sacramento, CA. Photograph courtesy the Sacramento City Cemetery.

schooners to cross rivers. The other seemingly safer but much longer options were by water vessel, around Cape Horn from New York or down the Isthmus of Panama, across it, and along the western coast to San Francisco—a trip that would take months.

Ironically, Hamilton's biggest danger by land was Indians, especially the dreaded Pawnee Tribe, who were described as a "thieving set of Devils." No one knows if Hamilton faced any Indian arrows on his trip, but he did witness the grand sight of buffalo herds covering hundreds of acres of land. Another man, named Dewolf, who also followed the Overland Trail westward, wrote about the buffalo sightings in his diary:

"To see thousands and thousands of them roaming and grazing over the vast plains and then shoot into them and see them run and bellow, fairly making the ground shake, is a grand sight."

Hamilton arrived in California to a scene of chaos. Wealth seekers and adventurers like himself crowded the camps like bees in a honeycomb, drunk with excitement over the prospects of striking it rich. They were hopelessly mistaken. Weakened by their efforts, which turned up few rewards, most found only desperation turning into despair. Hamilton was an educated and inventive man and not consumed by greed like others. He searched for black sand, which indicated the possibility of gold, and built a settlement known as Weaver Creek in the Bald Mountains. Within a year, he panned enough dust to make $12,000.

The following year, he was dead.

THE EXACT date of Hamilton's death in 1850 is still debated; even the month is challenged by differing accounts. Hamilton, like hundreds of gold seekers at the time, succumbed to the squalid conditions, contracted cholera, and never recovered. He reportedly passed away on a worn-out cot in a Sacramento hotel room. Samuel Rich, who ran the hotel known as Our Home, recalled "bringing him meals and waiting upon him." But in a short time he was gone. "All was done for him that lay in our power," Rich explained, "but, he passed away gently, far away from home and relatives." Rich initially listed the date of Hamilton's death as August 7 but later changed it to October 9.

Hamilton was buried in a trench alongside others who contracted the fatal disease. There was no marker, only a number. Hamilton's final resting place was simply known as tier 2, grave 50.

Five years after his death, a California man named Cyrus Woodman, described as "an old friend, but a political enemy," sought to put a gravestone were Hamilton was buried. He was told the Hamilton family was preparing a stone "in due time," but according to Edgar Hamilton, a nephew, "On account of the great distance and difficulty carrying out the plans," no stone was ever placed.

Nearly a quarter of a century later, Woodman, who was now living in Cambridge, Massachusetts, learned there was still no marker. In fact, he was told, the actual site of the grave was forgotten. Woodman sought out a man who worked with Hamilton in California and with great accuracy, it is said, the "old man" located the plot. Woodman ordered a stone, paid $106.80 out of his own pocket, and had it shipped by steamer to California, a trip that took nearly four months. In December of 1879, a tablet of polished Quincy granite arrived in Sacramento and was laid upon the site with the following inscription:

Colonel W. S. Hamilton
Born in New York August 4, 1797
Came to California in '49
Died October 9, 1850
In size and in talent and character, he
much resembled his illustrious father.
A friend erects this stone.

The tale of the stone is likely true, however, today a large monument stands as part of Hamilton Square on the grounds of the Old City Cemetery in Sacramento, the city's oldest interment site, where nearly 600 victims of the cholera epidemic are claimed to be buried. Captain John Sutter, who founded and named Sacramento, donated the land to the city and established the cemetery in 1849, the year before Hamilton died and around the same time many miners met their untimely ends. "[Hamilton] is the cemetery's most restless victim," city historians claim in a description of the current grave site. "He died once, was exhumed twice, and buried three times in three different locations." Hamilton's monument is simply marked, with his name and an inscription on the sides and in the front, a profile of his famous father. The date of death is listed as August 7, different than the October date Woodman had inscribed on the marker he sent from Massachusetts.

If Woodman's cross-country stone is laid somewhere, it's lost to time.

WILLIAM HAMILTON left no journal and kept no diary of his travels, so his life and adventures are up to others to explain. But they are few. In numerous biographies written about the life and legacy of his father, William is seldom mentioned. His brother, Phillip, who died by a dueler's bullet, understandably gets more attention. In fact, the only potential picture of William, referenced in several instances as such, may actually be his brother Philip.

There is only one book about William Hamilton, Sylvan J. Muldoon's account published in 1930, but even the title is indicative of his father's legacy: *Alexander Hamilton's Pioneer Son*. Muldoon was a bit of a pioneer himself, although in a totally different regard. He wrote several books on the metaphysical phenomenon known as "astral projection," or out-of-body experience (OBE), of which he had first-hand experience. His books are considered groundbreaking in the psychic and meditation world. So what compelled him to write about William Hamilton, the only non-paranormal themed book in his catalog? That's not known. Muldoon died in 1969. His work on Hamilton, however, is a straightforward account of a man who traveled far, influenced many, but left few words. There is not a single quote from Hamilton in the book. It's just a portrait of an individual who lived life on the edge and in the shadows at the same time. "He shunned all society," an anonymous acquaintance once said of Hamilton. "He adopted great plainness of garb, and while working in the mines lived and dressed more coarsely than any of his workmen. He would hardly have been recognized as the son of the greatest American Statesman, and one of the polished gentlemen of any period or century." Perhaps that assessment alone is why Hamilton left no lasting record of himself. The expectations of living up to his father's legacy were always present and demanding. He chose not to address or challenge it.

In Muldoon's book, Hamilton's exploits in the Wisconsin ore mines are better documented thanks to the Diggings, but his time in Peoria is not as detailed, perhaps figuring it wasn't as important. There are only a few paragraphs mentioning the Nomaque trial, Hamilton's involvement, and speculation too. As Muldoon asks, "Whether a sympathetic 'Bill' had anything to do with the Indian's escape is left for us to guess."

Hamilton did diligent work in Peoria, however, as a surveyor mapping out land for a city that would become the largest metropolis on the Illinois River; and as a lawyer, serving on the first murder trial in Peoria County, the first conviction, and, as it turned out, the first successful appeal. Several Illinois history books record this.

Thanks to the efforts of journalist Bill Moon, Nomaque's story also survives. After his escape and subsequent acquittal for murder, according to Moon, Nomaque was last seen in 1832 during Black Hawk's uprising and the battle of Stillman's Run, named for the militia leader, Major Isaiah Stillman, who engaged the tribes near Old Man's Creek after a parlay for peace failed. Nomaque was badly wounded in the battle. Although the number of killed on both sides is largely unknown, Stillman reportedly sent back a posse to check for some 53 of his own men who were still missing. As the story goes, and debated, several of Stillmen's honchos, who were said to be "Peorians," found the injured Nomaque on the battlefield and "humanely shot him to death to end his misery." If Nomaque was indeed in the Black Hawk War, William Hamilton, the man who once helped spare his life, would have been his adversary.

HAMILTON LEFT a lasting mark in Peoria. After establishing a map, which was later modified, the young surveyor was asked to make a distinction of the dirt pathways that led to several of the scattered hotels, saloons, and blacksmith shops in the burgeoning town. He named the dusty trail that ran alongside the river Water Street, and then paid homage to the men who worked by his father's side, despite their differences, and offered up these notables in respect: Washington, Adams, Jefferson, Madison, and Monroe.

All became street names in the newly plotted Peoria.

One can argue that Hamilton's idea to name the streets after the men who founded the nation was not an original one. Almost every United States city has streets named for these men. But in cities that "Billy" plotted and mapped, he proudly added one name out of respect. A lasting tribute from a son to a father he hardly knew but greatly admired. Today in Peoria, it's centrally located. Hamilton Boulevard runs east and west off Water Street and through the busy downtown business district.

Coincidently, on Hamilton Boulevard is the north side of the Peoria County Courthouse.

A PEORIA LOVE STORY

By the beginning of the third decade of the 20TH century, the Great Depression had consumed the industrial world and our nation. A country once rife with opportunity was reduced to hard-working families in desperation, even despair. The American Dream, which was booming in the Roaring '20s, began to unravel at the end of that decade. Many Americans were lured by the prospects of huge profits on Wall Street. Savings poured into stocks. Consumer buying slowed, spending dropped, and production ground down as goods went unsold. The stock market, however, continued to go up until it crashed under its own weight at the end of October 1929. In a panic, Americans lost faith in institutions to hold their money. They demanded it back. Banks were forced to liquidate in order to pay returns from reserves they did not have. Some mistakenly thought the bank run would stabilize, but it didn't. The banks went bankrupt. When the banks tanked, so did the economy. It was in this volatile climate that a relatively new invention called radio emerged. Even as the markets crashed and the Great Depression loomed, an estimated 12 million—or nearly 1 in every 10—households had a radio in it. Not a huge number, but it was growing. At any time of day, a turn of a knob would bring the current news, latest sports scores, president's speech, or just plain entertainment, like dramas or serials. It was like a newspaper in a box, gloriously simple and relatively cheap to buy. The programs themselves ranged in variety, but comedy serials were popular because they hit close to home, making an insufferable situation, like the Depression, seem comforting, bearable, and even humorous. Stars were born, including a married couple from Peoria, whose radio show became a national sensation. Peoria was an entertainment mecca, mostly in theaters and vaudeville shows that packed in the customers. A visit to "Will it Play?" Peoria was usually high on a theater performer's list of places to appear. Ironically, Peoria's most famous radio couple never worked at a station in the city. They grew up, met, and eventually married in Peoria, but they made their mark in show business elsewhere. Still, they were big stars in their hometown. It was an appreciation they reciprocated in their popular radio program about a couple with Midwestern roots. They never forgot where they came from. And years later, thanks to a picture magazine named *Look,* readers across the country were able to share in a very intimate moment: when the radio stars finally came home to say "thanks."

"AND NOW folks, get ready to smile again with radio's home folks, Vic and Sade...at whose small house half-way in the next block you are invited to spend a little while with at this time."

And with that sign-in began the most popular morning radio serial of its time.

Beginning in 1932, at 8:30 AM each day of the week except Sunday–even on Saturday for a time–the announcer's voice would welcome the *Vic and Sade* show. It was fun to listen, too. Technically it was a "soap opera," due to its primary audience of housewives who tuned in after the husbands went to work and the kids were off to school. But the show is remembered for being more than just a hokey romance or teary drama. Cleverly using colloquialisms and slang common for Midwesterners at the time, *Vic and Sade* humorously captured the voice of the working class and blue-collar spirit of Middle America. It was sponsored quite appropriately by the king of soap-makers and everyday household products, Procter & Gamble.

The show was a slow starter in terms of audience. After all, it was given a time slot where no one thought anybody would be listening. But eventually, for 15 minutes each day, more people tuned in. It wasn't quite like other popular daytime serials of the time, which carried dramatic storylines and cliffhanger endings over to each subsequent show; this was a new and original story each time, only with the same characters. Some radio historians today compare it to the hit TV show, *Seinfeld,* because it was always something about nothing, but done brilliantly.

The creator, writer, and mastermind of the *Vic and Sade* show knew a little something about Midwestern living. Paul Rhymer

was born in Fulton, Illinois, and as a small boy moved to Bloomington, right smack in the middle of the state. Bloomington became
the model for the show, and the characters Rhymer created were
based on real people he knew, like his neighbors or other people
he would see and observe every day, including the mail delivery
man, the garbage collector, the milk man, even the family doctor.
In the show, Rhymer gave them all silly names like I. Edison Box,
Gus Pink, and Dr. Bonebreaker. Some names playfully rhymed and
rolled off the tongue, like Rishigan Fishigan of Sishigan, Michigan, and still others were so twisted, listeners scratched their heads
in frustration.

The two main characters, Vic and Sade Gook, were a happily married couple who excitedly let the world and all its silly provisions
come to their house on Virginia Street, where most of the scenes
took place. Rhymer parodied just about everything he remembered
about growing up in a small town, like the Elks Club and other
lodges his father attended or the grocery store where his mother
shopped. There were a few gags, but it was mostly dialogue and
Rhymer's ingenious use of words that drove the scenes, all spoken
with a downhome Midwestern drawl. The rest of America would
laugh right along.

The poet Edgar Lee Masters praised Rhymer's writing, calling
the show "the best American humor of its day," and others even
went so far as to compare its witty satirical humor to Mark Twain.

That's high praise for a show hardly mentioned today. Don't fault
the actors or Rhymer, who got most of the credit. The problem is
Vic and Sade never made it past noon. The show ran successfully
for 14 years starting the day off with a laugh, like a TV morning talk
show might today, but the most popular radio shows by audience
size were on in the evening and usually only once a week, similar
to network television sitcoms.

Vic and Sade never got there.

But another Midwest couple portrayed on the radio did.

On Tuesday nights, from a fictional place called Wistful Vista,
audiences couldn't get enough of *Fibber McGee and Molly.*

This is their story.

MAYBE IT was that lively jig that did the trick. Or that deep, lovely singing voice, a contralto–the lowest range for a female–that really stood out. Whatever it was that caught Jim Jordan's fancy that December, 1915, night in Peoria, Illinois, he was smitten. But he was also very shy. So he convinced a pal to introduce him to the young lady named Marian.

Jim Jordan grew up on a farm just outside of Peoria. "Half of the kids were farmers and the other half were coal miners," he recalled. Most kids in Jim's class dropped out of school to help with chores on the farm or pull coal from the mines during the winter months. Jim found another way. "I had an advantage. I would sing for someone and get a job."

Jim was especially fond of his father, who entertained the Jordan siblings, four boys and three girls, by telling wildly exaggerated stories. He had a captive audience. Before getting married, one story went, "I ventured down south (to Texas) to skin buffalo and make a little side money." The story was true, but the elder Jordan would spice it up a bit by explaining how he survived dangerous hunts alongside the famous Buffalo Bill. Jim would listen and learn.

Jim sang and acted in plays at his small school near Kickapoo, Illinois. Then, at the age of 12, he enjoyed a career break of sorts: Jim's dad packed up the Jordan brood and moved to Peoria. The big city was only a few miles away, but it meant so much more to an aspiring young actor. "There was always something magical about Peoria," he later recalled in a 1984 interview with Wally Gair, a fellow broadcaster and radio historian, who graduated from Bradley University in Peoria and for a time taught the history of broadcasting there. Perhaps knowing Gair personally, Jordan opened up–about his career, his marriage and the radio phenomenon known as *Fibber McGee and Molly.* It all got off to a rolling start, he remembered, once he got to the big city. "In vaudeville, burlesque, and road shows, performers couldn't wait to get to Peoria," Jordan said.

Theaters like the Hippodrome, Madison, Majestic, Orpheum, and Rialto were brimming with flashing marquee lights and lines stretching out the door. Peoria had a reputation as a "bad show town," a term of endearment among vaudeville entertainers who challenged themselves to come to Peoria and not fail, or "lay eggs," as others warned. The audiences were tough. "There was a lot of life there then," Jim said. "It was a wide-open town—pretty wild."

But Jim was just a teenager, and school came first. He went to St. Mark's Elementary and later Spalding Institute. He perfected his craft in school plays but now on a much larger scale. "I carried a spear, more or less, but it was pretty exciting," he remembers.

Then, in 1915, during a Christmas choir practice at St. John's Church on Peoria's south side, Jim saw Marian Driscoll, a "pretty blue-eyed, brown haired, slightly freckled" coal miner's daughter who played piano, violin, and loved to sing. "Introduce me to her," the reserved Jim asked a friend.

They met and liked each other, but Jim was too shy to escort her home that night, or even ask. Eventually he got the nerve. They spent more time together and soon fell in love. Then, much to the disappointment of Marian's parents, Jim dropped out of school and joined a touring vocal group. In 1917, he left for Chicago to pursue a singing career. But he was homesick for Marian. So he returned to Peoria and went to work at the post office.

World War I was on, and Jim was on the draft list. So far, he hadn't been called. He wanted to ask Marian to marry him but feared his number would come up. It was August, 1918. "The war is winding down," a friend insisted. "You'll never be called. Go ahead and get married." So they did. Their honeymoon was a trip to St. Louis to visit Marian's sister. That's when the summons came. Jim was going to France.

The war was easy on Jim. He put in six weeks at an artillery boot camp in Florida and was shipped off as a staff sergeant with the 122ND Engineers. As soon as they landed overseas, Jim got sick and spent the rest of his tour in army hospitals. While recovering, he put together a musical group called The Premiere Review, and through the army's entertainment division, they performed for troops at U.S. hospitals in France. "There were two quartets," Jim explains. "One was an evening-close type, singing, you know, classics and so on, straight standup thing. The other was the comedy quartet, real slapstick or real lowdown.

"It was a great show," he added, "fine people."

Meanwhile, back home in Peoria, Marian taught piano and waited.

Shortly after the war ended, Jim returned to Marian and worked odd jobs before deciding to get back into show-biz, this time as a couple. They accepted small gigs, made little money, but were determined. Then, by chance, an advance man for a theater company heard them sing. He told the couple they had a shot. Jim was excited. He had an idea, a venture really, that involved touring with a revue company. A bigger show meant bigger towns and bigger profits. They needed to hire musicians and singers and purchase equipment, but they were hopelessly short of cash.

They mortgaged their home and sold their old car, but it wasn't enough. Then Jim's aunt offered to help. Now with the needed funds, The Metropolitan Musical Entertainers was launched. Jim sang tenor while Marian played piano. A slew of other artists joined in, offering all kinds of musical entertainment complete with a "big band sound" filled by fiddles, xylophones, saxophone, French horn, and bell ringers. "Musical Novelties," the posters read. "An Engagement Extraordinary."

The work was rewarding, but the long hours and days on the road were exhausting. "You know you want to be in show business," Jim says, "but you don't tell everybody because in those days there's nothing honorable about being in show business. You know, you didn't brag about it."

The group toured by train and performed in dance halls, vaudeville theaters, high schools—wherever they could find an audience. Sometimes, in larger venues, Jim would give a lecture on the various instruments used. The concert act worked for a time. Then Marian got pregnant and went home to Peoria to raise a daughter, Kathryn.

Jim stayed on with the traveling troupe, but he eventually returned to his wife and new baby. To make ends meet, he worked low-paying jobs, first as a dry-goods store clerk, then in the toy section of a local department store. He and Marian did a few singing engagements together, but money was tight. It was during this time that Jim was discovered by a couple of prominent songwriters and musicians from Chicago. They invited him to come to the big city and sing their tunes. Although somewhat disheartened by past ventures into the show-biz world, Jim went along.

Jim and Marian Jordan as "Fibber McGee and Molly." Photograph courtesy Culver Pictures, Inc.

Chicago was where the action was. The studios were bigger, the paychecks were larger, and something new was just starting to crackle through the airwaves: radio. Although it was new, untested, and a bit of a gamble, the choice was clear for aspiring artists—radio was the place to be.

Jim and Marian Jordan would soon find that out. Thanks to radio, the husband and wife team from Peoria would become more successful than either could ever have imagined as a fictional, but somewhat truthful, couple named Fibber McGee and Molly.

RADIO WAS uniquely American. True, the idea of using radio waves rather than wires to transmit messages was developed by international inventors in the late 19TH century—Italy's Marconi is most widely credited—but radio was a technology that truly experienced synchronous development. The first radio station is attributed to a man named Charles Herrold, from California, who in 1909 coined the phrase "broadcasting," previously being used by farmers to describe the "tossing of seeds." Another American, Edwin Armstrong, is credited with inventing frequency modulation, or FM, but that would come later. The first commercially licensed radio broadcast in the U.S. began in 1920. By 1928, there were three national radio networks.

The 1920s began with new ideas and roaring optimism. There was steady work and decent pay. Items were being mass-produced, like automobiles, that had seemed out of reach for most middle-class families but were now built with greater comfort and efficiency, and most importantly, at a price that was "affordable to anyone." Comparatively, radios were moderately priced considering its inventiveness, and manufacturers, sensing a growing need, kept the cost low and the demand high.

The nation enjoyed a period of ebullient hope in the 1920s. By the start of the next decade, however, it was gone. The stock market raced upward until the end of October 1929, when it all came to a screeching halt. In 1933, the Great Depression bottomed out.

Radio, however, became more popular than ever. And its usefulness became apparent too. During the crisis, President Hoover took to the airwaves to assure the nation the markets would rebound. Don't panic, he instructed. But it was too late. Radio had sent a clear message across the country, albeit a damaging one.

Despite the financial gloom, radio was something everyone could share. A standard table model was around $20 (about $200 today) and the hours of entertainment it provided were free, although advertisers were hoping otherwise. The appeal outweighed the initial cost. Soon, Americans not only wanted a radio in the house, they wanted one in every room.

Thanks to radio's rise, stars were born, celebrities made, and talent exposed.

It was a great time to be a performer.

Like Jim and Marian Jordan.

WHEN JIM went to Chicago for work, Marian often made the trek from Peoria to visit. There they would stay at Jim's brother Byron's house in a cozy neighborhood on the city's north side called Rogers Park. One night, while excitedly listening to "the box" in the living room, Byron heard a woman singing. "You can do better," he told Marian. So Jim and Marian decided to give it a try. They auditioned for a local radio station manager and were hired for six months at $10 a week. Their first show was all singing, no talking. "We didn't speak a word," Jim recalled. "It was all songs and piano." It also didn't get much attention, but Jim didn't mind. "That's when a performer learned how [to do it]," he said. "Because you knew nobody was listening to it anyway, so you caught on how to do it."

The radio gig wasn't paying the bills, so they kept performing on stage. To promote their next appearance, they continued to broadcast the radio show. While performing at the Palace Theater in Chicago, they met another musical couple who suggested they add some comedy to their act. Jim kept insisting they were musicians, not comedians, but he went along with the idea, hoping for a break.

They added some storytelling and banter to their stage act and auditioned for another radio company. They were hired to host a children's show on WENR. Marian especially took to it. Mimicking her daughter's constant "chattering," she experimented with voices, raising her tone to sound like a child, using her "teeny" voice, as she called it. Jim also perfected an "old man" act, one who told exaggerated stories, like his father used to do. They often played off a group of children who could be heard in the background, giggling and clapping with glee.

"We did everything under the sun during those years," Jim remembers fondly. "My God, we did everything. We worked."

Suddenly the Jordans were in high demand. They appeared on several shows, sometimes together, sometimes as actors on other serials. *The Smith Family,* a drama about a typical middle-class American family, gave Marian her big break, playing the leading role as the mother of the Smith clan. Jim played the prize-fighting boyfriend of her fictional daughter. When the radio characters married, Jim played the son-in-law to his real-life wife. No one in the audience knew. The show became a breakout hit, and Jim and Marian picked up many new listeners and fans.

The Jordans' first radio show as a comedy act was called *Smackout,* about the proprietor of a country store somewhere in rural America. Jim's character, Luke Grey, would always say he was "smack out" of this and "smack out" out of that, but he always had a tall tale to share. Marian played a variety of characters, using different voices like the "teeny" voice for a little girl who liked to talk to her dolly. She appropriately named the character "Teeny." The show ran for three years, while Jim and Marian did guest spots on other programs. Their repertoire of nearly 150 voices on *Smackout* was getting noticed by other show producers and sponsors. "You got paid by how many voices you did," Jim remembers, "not anything else."

The Johnson Wax Company was looking for a showcase endorsement and asked the Jordans to come up with something new. Jim wasn't sure about keeping the *Smackout* character or format, so they pitched the idea of playing a middle-aged couple, possibly touring the country by vehicle, an easy tie-in to the car wax company.

It was suggested Jim's voice was already well-known to listeners as the man who tells "tall-tales," so writers and producers wanted to keep that theme but change the setting. They needed a name that fit. Jim's name supposedly came from a writer who suggested *Fibber* for the first name and *McGee* for the last. Jim liked it. Marian's character was supposedly named after an old Irish song, *Molly Oh, Molly Oh.* Jim claims they had the idea for years: "Molly was the name Marian and I had for a long time. That was an Irish name and a good-sounding name, and we said whenever the right thing comes along we'd use it."

It finally came along.

Jim and Marian Jordan went to New York City and, with an act playfully exploiting an espoused couple's follies, they became Fibber McGee and Molly.

SOUND: HANDCLAPS

ANNCR: *And once again, it's Fibber McGee and Molly time. Fibber McGee and Molly, the dramatic story of a woman with her faith in a man, and a man with his faith in a newspaper. Will something exciting, unusual, or momentous take place in the little frame house at seventy-nine Wistful Vista tonight? Or is that expecting too much? Yes, I guess it's expecting too much. Anyway, here they are, Fibber McGee and Molly!*

The plot of the show was simple. Fibber would tell tall-tales or dream up wildly elaborate schemes and Molly would playfully dispute them. In the early shows, Fibber was portrayed as an out-of-luck ne'er-do-well, but later became more of a foolish jester who should know better, but ignores logical advice. Fibber's antics usually led to hilarious gags, mostly pratfalls where something simple suddenly goes awry. "It's been one of those days. Everything's gone wrong," Fibber would explain after forgetting to turn off the main water valve and flooding the basement. Molly would usually sit back and let Fibber play the bumbler, always lovingly of course, and usually with a good quip to put him in his place. Oftentimes, there was a surprise or trick ending, but always a happy one.

The overstuffed closet became their signature bit. Jim recalls, "One day accidently we had in the script that this guy [Fibber] was such a slob that he went to the closet and opened it up and it showed how slovenly he was, and so out of order of everything, and the stuff came crashing out of it."

Actually, the first show that introduced the closet was in March of 1939. Fibber was trying to find a dictionary to look up a word. He asked Molly.

"It's probably in the closet with the rest of your stuff," she explained.

Fibber smartly explained back that all his stuff was in the closet, "arranged in there just the way I want it." Besides, he added, the door was locked. "You don't think I would leave all my personal stuff layin' around for any prowler [to steal]," he told her.

Molly tried the latch and it clicked. "McGee...it isn't locked," she said, swinging the door open.

Loud thuds and clatter could be heard as box after box, presumably one bigger than the other, tumbled to the floor.

"I'm buried alive!" Molly said. "Get this junk off me."

It was a laugh riot, both in the studio and for the audience. That's when a light went off in Jim's head. "Gee, maybe that's a running [gag]," he thought. "We tried it again and that was the beginning of the closet."

From that point on, everybody waited for the closet to open. "Got so people came to see that done," Jim said, referring to the live studio audience. "We had an eight-foot stepladder that he, the sound man on stage, would pile the stuff on. He had it piled meticulously so it would make that sound when he tipped it. He'd just tip it like a domino effect, you know. It was funny to have—the biggest thing that happened on one of the biggest shows of radio was a sight gag."

Thanks in part to that closet gag, the clever writing, and the ingenius comic timing of Jim and Marian Jordan, *Fibber McGee and Molly* was a huge hit. The show became a staple on Tuesday nights and built a loyal following, like the *Vic and Sade* show did in the

Back in Peoria, the Jordans revisit their old home and classroom.

PAGES 132, 135, 136: First printed in *Look* Magazine (April 25, 1950, Vol. 14 No. 9), reproduced from author's personal collection. Photographs by Earl Theisen.

mornings. Audiences just couldn't get enough of their favorite Midwestern couples on the radio. Listeners of both shows may also have recognized the voice of Bernadine Flynn, who appeared on several *Fibber McGee and Molly* programs and later became Sade on the *Vic and Sade* show.

But despite the Midwestern connection, the structure of the *Fibber McGee and Molly* show was vastly different from *Vic and Sade*. Like Paul Rhymer, the writer for *Vic and Sade*, the brains behind *Fibber McGee and Molly* was Don Quinn, who wrote all of the program's scripts. But since the *Fibber McGee and Molly* show was full of physical gags, the stunts were just as important as the words. Jim and Marian had to mimic and sell the bits, not just read them. Oftentimes, they would help create the illusions by playing off actual props, like broomsticks and lamps. The actors were the reason America loved *Fibber McGee and Molly*, while the writer justifiably got most of the credit for the *Vic and Sade* show.

That may be part of the reason why *Vic and Sade* is hardly a go-to reference when discussing old-time radio programs today. Only radio historians, purists, and archivists agree it holds its own among the greats. For others, sadly, it's forgotten. Even Rhymer seemed to downplay its importance; for years after the show ended he was so moved and flattered by admirers that when he received letters from fans asking about certain shows and dialogue, he responded by sending them the original type-written scripts. He must have figured no one else wanted them.

The name *Fibber McGee and Molly*, however, is forever a part of American pop culture.

IN FEBRUARY 1950, after nearly 30 years in the business and a weekly radio audience of 40 million, Jim and Marian Jordan came back to Peoria. A picture magazine called *Look* asked the couple to do it. It's easy to see why *Look* was interested in a story of the radio stars coming home. The founder of the magazine was a man named Gardner Cowles, who grew up in Algona, Iowa, went to Harvard to study business and journalism, returned to his Midwest roots in the mid-1920s, and began working for the *Des Moines Register* and the *Des Moines Tribune,* both newspapers started by his father. Along with his brother, John, also a newspaperman in the family, Cowles was convinced that another national picture magazine like *Life* would be successful. He was right. Before getting into the magazine business, however, in the 1930s, Cowles and his brother bought and ran several radio stations, mostly in the Midwest. Perhaps that's why *Look* was especially kind to the radio stars of the day, with features and photo vignettes. Radio was perfect for a picture magazine. After all, who didn't want to *see* their favorite radio stars up close and in action? Cowles was from the Midwest. So perhaps he had a soft spot for performers that came from cities like Peoria, an entertainment magnet in the middle of the heartland.

The Jordans had gone back to Peoria before to visit friends and family, but they had done so discreetly and never under the guise of the radio couple. Cowles had an idea. The *Look* photographers would follow the Jordans around town and capture their reactions, others' reactions, and any mischief that followed. Jim and Marian would, in essence, be *Fibber McGee and Molly*, hobnobbing around town, playfully interacting and generally enjoying the attention of their adoring fans. A feature in the magazine would follow.

It was classic showmanship by *Look*, and the Jordans didn't disappoint. *Back to Peoria with Fibber McGee and Molly* featured 17 photographs and just as many hilarious captions, including one shot of Jim trying to lift Marian through the door of their old house. The caption reads: "He couldn't lift me over the threshold the first time either." Marian has an infectious smile on her face, while Jim playfully struggles.

The Jordans visited the place they first met, St. John's Church, and their old schools. The kids and staff were thrilled to see their favorite radio stars up close and in person. "We haunted the old haunts," Jim said.

Marian joined in with the choir as Jim sat at his old desk, "dreaming up the tall tales that influenced his hookey and network ratings."

Marian's sister, Nell, and some of her nine brothers still lived in Peoria. "I enjoyed the reunion," Jim said. "It was one of the few times the boys didn't beat me up on sight."

They both agreed Peoria had changed quite a bit since they were youngsters, but added that all the changes have been for the better. "Peoria landmarks seemed just about the same," Marian said. "The old newspaper seller said to Jim, 'Howdy, Jordan, still working at the post office?'"

"They live in a ranch house in Encino," the *Look* article read when it ran several months later, "but Peoria is still hometown, and almost every year they manage to get back to visit."

But this trip was special.

"This year, they went back again, to see relatives, the old gang, the old quartet, the old opera house, their honeymoon house and to pull taffy and bob for apples," the article continued. In it, more pictures recorded the moments. Like Jim with Peoria Mayor Joe

Jim and Marian Jordan's
visit to Peoria in February
1950 for *Look* magazine.
SEE PAGE 132 FOR CITATION.

Malone at the barber shop, Marian pouring tea at the Hotel Pere
Marquette, and both doing that famous jig of Marian's on the stage
of the Orpheum Theater, where Jim explained, "You can still see
the marks where the missiles went wide."

The Jordans were everywhere, and the town loved it.

"We don't want to appear upstage," Marian told a newspaper
reporter who attributed the quote to "Molly," "but we cannot get
around to see all the people we would like to."

As it turned out, the people would come out to see them.

On the night of February 15, the Jordans were honored guests of
Bradley University and the basketball team their show co-sponsored.
The McGee team was playing the Caterpillar Diesels at the Robertson Memorial Field House. And while the invite had a specific
purpose, it also was a good opportunity for Peorians to see their
hometown stars in the flesh, and, as it turned out, do their radio
act too. When the starting line-ups where read, the booming loud-
speaker voice announced, quite puzzlingly, that "Fibber McGee"
was one of the starting five players. The crowd roared in approval. Jim flat-footed it about the raised court, pointing to his knee
pads—on backwards—and his football shoulder pads. "As a basketball player," the papers teased, "he made a good comedian—and he
knew it." A mock minute of play was interrupted by Fibber, now
playing the part of the referee, blowing his whistle incessantly.

"I sure hope none of our boys fall off that elevated floor," Jim

Jim Jordan addresses the crowd at the Robertson Memorial Field House on the campus of Bradley University. SEE PAGE 132 FOR CITATION.

playfully told a reporter before the game. "When I was a boy, we were lucky to find a barn for a court and barrel hoops for baskets."

At halftime, Fibber introduced Molly. She was "strictly herself," the papers noted, referring to her lovable character. "How do you do, I'm sure," she said, greeting the packed house. The pair put on a quick radio program "live."

"Oh, Heavenly Days," Molly said to the crowd's delight as Fibber taunted her with jokes. "T'aint funny, McGee," she added.

On a more serious note, the university had plans to induct the radio couple as honorary members of the Bradley Braves Bivouac for their efforts in furthering athletics at the campus. Seizing the moment, Fibber and Molly let the follies fly. They "coughingly smoked" the Braves mascot's peace pipe and donned the headdress, the papers reported. Then they wrapped themselves in the celebratory school blanket. The basketball game was second fiddle to America's favorite couple and the crowd ate it up...every second.

That's because Peoria had become a part of their radio act. "We had a lot of references to Peoria," Jim recalled. "Fibber would talk about Main Street hill, canoeing on the Illinois River, and various characters in town."

MOLLY: *What's that little key there for?*
FIBBER: *Uh, well, that's a padlock key?*
MOLLY: *What padlock?*
FIBBER: *Well, for the backyard gate we used to have in Peoria.*
MOLLY: *What are ya keepin' that for? Are ya homesick?*
FIBBER: *No, but if we ever moved back to Peoria, I'd try to rent the same house 'cause this key fits the padlock there. You gotta think ahead in these things.*

The trip to Peoria and the *Look* article, which appeared that following April, turned out to be an opportunity for the Jordans to say "thank you" to their hometown fans and, in retrospect, goodbye. Although they didn't know it at the time, it would be their last public appearance together in Peoria.

The show's monster ratings were finally starting to crack, and the country was changing in ways that *Fibber McGee and Molly,* the radio program, was not. The rise of television was pushing radio aside. The "image," it was said, was forging ahead of the "word" in home entertainment. Many radio stars saw a good opportunity in television and switched, but the Jordans wanted both.

A month after visiting Peoria, Jim and Marian shot a pilot for NBC television. The cast gathered around microphones, reading from a script. It was basically the radio show filmed. But it was never picked up by the network, and Jim became disinterested with switching mediums. "Tv devours talent," he later said, not the least bit envious of those who made the move and found success on television. "Its impact is so great that the audiences get tired of you ten times faster than in radio."

The Jordans were determined to see the radio show through to the end. In the fall of 1953, their determination was rewarded. The network changed the format of the show, and *Fibber McGee and Molly* became a quarter-hour program that aired five nights a week rather than just on Tuesday. The show also ran on weekends as part of NBC's *Weekend Monitor* series that played various radio show snippets continuously from early Saturday morning to midnight Sunday. The Jordans recorded all new material for their 10 five-minute vignettes each weekend, the equivalent of two half-hour

shows. Each segment had a new sponsor. "We sold them like eggs,
I guess, by the crate," Jim would later recall.

Six years later, it ended.

WHEN THE last *Fibber McGee and Molly* segment aired on September 6, 1959, a 24-year radio institution was over. Ironically, the
program was about Fibber and Molly imagining themselves as TV
stars. As it turned out, however, they weren't imagining.

On September 15, 1959, just a little over a week after the final
Fibber McGee and Molly radio program aired, America's favorite
couple from Wistful Vista were back on the air, this time on television. Jim and Marian Jordan, however, were not. Despite objections from the radio show producers, NBC went ahead with a TV
show starring Bob Sweeny and Cathy Lewis, two former cast members on the radio show, as Fibber and Molly. It ran for 26 episodes
before being dropped.

By then, the Jordans were enjoying being away from the daily
grind of producing a radio show. They took a few vacations and
relaxed, but mostly enjoyed the time they spent with their grand-
children. Then, in 1960, the network asked them back to once
again produce segments for the *Weekend Monitor.* If they had any
thoughts of returning, Marian's health changed their minds.

Although she had suffered minor complications from an illness
that briefly sidelined her in 1937, a recent visit to the doctor revealed
something much more serious: a malignant tumor in her ovary.
Time was short. The Jordans turned down the network offer and
spent the next year in quiet seclusion at their home in California.
On Friday, April 6, 1961, with her family bedside her, Marian Jordan slipped away. She was eight days short of turning 63.

Jim was heartbroken and announced his retirement from show
business on the *Jack Paar Show* later that year. He spent the next
nine years out of the limelight, mostly traveling. Time began to
heal his grief. During a trip to Hawaii, he met a woman, a former
acquaintance, fell in love, and eventually remarried. No longer
alone and feeling peppier after fully recovering from open-heart
surgery in the winter of 1970, Jordan decided it was time to get
back in the spotlight. He appeared on several programs (mostly

radio nostalgia shows), announced commercials, voiced animated characters, and did personal appearances. His appearances were usually greeted by accolades of the past, specifically his years as Fibber. In 1983, a bronze star bearing the name *Fibber McGee and Molly* was unveiled on Hollywood's Walk of Fame. Jim was there.

Five years later, on April 1, 1988, Jim Jordan died at the age of 91.

Although the *Fibber McGee and Molly* show had been off the air for more than three decades, the news of Jim's passing was the top story in the Peoria paper the next day. "He was the son of a farmer, who aspired to be a singer and she was a coal miner's daughter who wanted to teach music," the *Journal Star* wrote in tribute to its former hometown stars.

Even today, the name *Fibber McGee and Molly* is synonymous with Peoria. More so, some would say, than the fictional radio town of Wistful Vista. *Look* magazine knew it. On the cover of the edition featuring the Jordans' homecoming were simply these words: *"Fibber McGee and Molly* in Peoria." No other explanation was needed.

Maybe it was their Midwest sentimentally that made the act work so well. It certainly kept the audience wanting more. An audience that could only sit in front of their radios and laugh along at the misfortunes of a married couple struggling to make ends meet, scheming up ways to try and make life better, and more often than not getting in each other's way trying.

Behind the scenes it was a different story. At the end of each radio program, in secret, and never revealed to their listeners, Jim and Marian Jordan, AKA Fibber McGee and Molly, would silently hold hands.

A Peoria love story.

"Goodnight, y'all," Molly would say, signing off.

THEME MUSIC UP

GUARD THE MAIL

In Dayton, Ohio, on March 23, 1913, after a deluge of rain that lasted a full two days, the Great Miami River, a long tributary of the Ohio River, swelled and breached the crude levees designed to hold it back. The town of Dayton was decimated as rushing waters turned streets into fast-moving rapids and fires caused by ruptured gas lines burned uncontrollably above the water line. Just about everything in the city was ruined. The town became a virtual wasteland. When the waters finally receded, a search to find lost items commenced and several large crates were found buried deep in the muck and mire. Inside were mostly pieces of long pine sticks and fabric sheets. A couple of bicycle shop owners, brothers, had stored them away, hoping one day their significance would be lauded. The crates contained the body and wings of an aircraft that 10 years earlier had flown a man nearly a minute off the ground. It was on December 17, 1903, in a North Carolina coastal town called Kitty Hawk, when a handful of handpicked spectators watched Orville and Wilbur Wright's homemade flyer make that momentous flight. Among them was a man who worked at a lifesaving station nearby and was recruited to help the brothers carry the parts to the hill. He was handed a bulky camera and became the Wright's impromptu photographer. Afterward, a skeptical public was unimpressed. There were only somewhat blurry pictures and a few eyewitness accounts to mark the occasion. Humans could fly, the Wrights had proved, just not very efficiently and, so far, not publicly. The Wrights bided their time and let others build flying machines that also went short distances and amazed crowds. Then, in 1908, in Le Mans, France, just outside of Paris, the Wrights sent a modified flyer into the air that not only stayed aloft for several minutes but also did turns and navigated an impossible figure-eight. It even landed where it took off. A crowd of hundreds cheered. Later that year, they flew a plane more than 76 miles in two-plus hours. The Wrights had done it. The age of flight was a reality. Around the same time, Charles Lindbergh was six years old and living on a farm in Minnesota. In 1909, he heard a buzzing sound coming from his bedroom window. It was an engine, for sure, but not a car. He climbed through the window and onto the roof. There he marveled as a Wright-inspired flyer swooped over his head. The future aviator was hooked: "Afterward, I remember lying in the grass and looking at the clouds and thinking how much fun it would be to fly up there among the clouds." Of course, the young Lindbergh would grow up to become an aviation legend, but like the Wright Brothers, whose early accomplishments were mostly ignored until later, the most dangerous flight of Lindbergh's career wasn't the one over the Atlantic, when everyone was looking. It was flying over the cornfields of Illinois, when no one noticed.

CHARLES LINDBERGH didn't have to do it. He could have refused. It was February, 1928, not quite a year removed from his historic record-breaking flight over the Atlantic, and the 27-year-old aviator, the most famous pilot in the world and quite possibly the most recognizable person on the planet, was about to jump into a rickety biplane again and fly the airmail over Illinois.

It had been a whirlwind ride for the modest Lindbergh since his endurance flight across the ocean that ended triumphantly in Paris on May 21, 1927. It started quite literally overseas. "He has chatted with kings and queens and has been showered with the plaudits of the people in more than a score of countries," the papers declared, just hours after the flight. "He has sat with the mighty; has dined with royal blood, and found reception in courts where only the feet of the great have trodden." Lindbergh bravely took it all in.

Back home, it was the same, but more so: Lindbergh was a national hero. After the honorary ticker-tape parade in New York City and meeting with the President, Lindbergh went on a multiple-city tour to "publicize air travel," he insisted. But the adoring crowds only wanted more of "Lucky Lindy." From the summer of 1927 until October of that same year, the "hero" pilot logged more than 22,000 miles, led parades in 82 different cities, and stayed at least one night in each of the continental 48 states. An estimated 30 mil-

Charles A. Lindbergh.
Photograph courtesy the
Library of Congress.

lion people turned out to see him, about a quarter of the nation's total population.

Typical of his workmanlike style, Lindbergh had only one stipulation he personally used for motivation as he traveled from one destination to the next, a trait he learned while mundanely flying the airmail over Illinois' small towns and cornfields day in and day out. *Be on time,* he silently insisted to himself during each flight.

But by the beginning of 1928, Lindbergh was getting tired and just plain sick of all the attention. "There should be no celebrity without a purpose," he said, hoping to quell the crowds that greeted him wherever he showed up. Even hotel bathrooms weren't safe from gawkers. He later admitted that while he loved the flying, the crowds and celebrity were a chore he grew to hate. So in February of 1928, when the famous pilot should have been searching for a place to escape, he agreed to another publicity stunt, this time to appease a former employer and make one last ceremonial run on his old mail route. On February 20, a Monday, he would make a stop in Peoria, Illinois—to pick up the mail.

Thousands would be waiting to greet him.

LINDBERGH WAS no stranger to Peoria. His daily mail drop—oftentimes delayed by weather or tardy mailbags—allowed him to mingle with locals during stopovers. Many who lived near the airstrips remember the young flyer kindly accepting lunch invitations before loading up and blasting off again, sometimes in conditions not fit for an eagle's flight. Lindbergh was modest, polite, and always worried—not so much about the weather (although that was a concern) but whether he could deliver the mail on time. That was his job. He always had a deadline to meet and cargo to protect.

For Lindbergh, the ceremonial mail flight was a favor to the Robertson Air Company of St. Louis, which was contracted by the government to fly CAM-2, the route across Illinois between Springfield and Chicago. The honorary flight would stress the need for airmail, something Lindbergh greatly admired; the importance of service contracts to struggling airlines, like RAC; and support for its brave pilots, Lindbergh's friends, who were still making the dangerous rounds every day and for little pay, considering the risk. It's a business trip, plain and simple, Lindbergh modestly said before agreeing to the stunt.

The papers soon got word that at each stop there would be "no ceremony, no speech-making and no ostentatious display, other than the cheers from the multitude." Lindy had insisted "the trip up and back be as free from show as possible," the *Peoria Star* reported.

But the ceremony turned serious and considerably more important when the government saw a good opportunity to make promotional use of Lindbergh's favor flight. Fancy commemorative postcards were printed, which for a few cents would go to support the U.S. Postal Service, the airmail service, and for senders and receivers alike, provide a keepsake to remember, since Lindbergh's sign-off would be on each and every parcel. The postcards sold out in just hours, and on the day of Lindbergh's flight, the mail came in bundles, piles of it, many with notes or writing on the outside of the envelopes asking if that particular letter could be carried on Lindy's plane.

Now, as the mail stacked up, the day had even more significance— the largest volume of letters by number and weight ever to be delivered by air.

Lindy was about to break another record.

He also needed more planes. So he recruited his old buddy pilots who were still on the Midwest circuit, and on Monday, February

20, as mechanics cocked the propellers and the engines whirred to life, four Douglas biplanes, led by the most famous pilot in the world, readied for takeoff from Robertson's Field in St. Louis. They were due in Peoria around 6 o'clock that evening. The crowds were already starting to arrive.

By dusk, those who braved the "chilly temperatures" and fought off "frost bite," as the papers reported, strained their eyes skyward and listened. At first, they could only hear the sound of purring engines in the distance. Then, suddenly, small dots appeared on the horizon. As the engine sounds grew louder, faint silhouettes of the four biplanes effortlessly flying overhead appeared. The crowd cheered as the mechanical birds lowered and circled the 10,000 or so faithful who waited behind a line of National Guardsmen keeping a fair distance between the massive crowd and the dirt airstrip of Varney Field on Peoria's northwest side, also known as Big Hollow Field. Flares that lined the strip cast an eerie glow.

Which one is Lindy? the crowd wondered. The planes all looked the same: red with a white strip on the wing, the word ROBERTSON on the side, and, in bold letters, U.S. MAIL painted near the tail.

Which one is Lindy?

A reporter noted that a small child said out loud, "Lindy flies with one wing," remembering the *Spirit of St. Louis* from pictures. But all the aircraft in the sky were "bi-wings," another in the crowd corrected.

One plane broke free from the loose formation and pulled ahead. The pilot made a sharp turn, descended, and gracefully touched the earth, sending dirt clouds and several flares tumbling like lit matchsticks across the field. The crowd went wild. "It's him," one man shouted. As the throng surged forward, the Guardsmen who stood rigidly at attention with "bayonets drawn" couldn't help but turn to take a look. As they marveled with the others at the spectacle of Lindbergh's plane on the ground, about a hundred spectators "broke ranks" and ran for the field. The Guardsmen were hopelessly outmatched.

From high above, Lindbergh could see the landscaped dotted with parked vehicles and thousands of heads, hats, and waving arms. The sound of the cheers was drowned out by the incessant whine of

Lindbergh commemora-
tive postcard and 10¢ *Spirit
of St. Louis* stamp, February 21, 1928. From author's
personal collection.

the engine and whistling wind, but Lindbergh sensed their enthu-
siasm. The plan was for his plane to land first, followed by the three
others. Lindbergh's reception would take only minutes. He would
be greeted by the local dignitaries, pick up the mailbags, and be off
with the three other pilots, also picking up bags, following behind.

As Lindbergh came in for the landing, he noticed a small group,
about a hundred or so, holding onto their hats and running like a
herd of hurried buffalo towards the airstrip. Lindbergh frantical-
ly waved them off as "though each member was a giant that would
tear his plane to pieces," the paper remarked. He taxied toward the
reception area, but quickly changed his mind. At that point, the
pilot "was in no mood for invitations." He remained in his seat and
motioned for a policeman to get within shouting distance of the
plane. "I thought you were going to keep the people back," Lindbergh bellowed, chastising the baffled officer. The policeman could
only shrug. Then, with the engine still humming, Lindbergh "gave
her the gun" and quickly turned the plane around, "throwing dust
into the face of his tormentors."

"The intrepid 100 or more," the papers reported, "mopped the
dirt out of their eyes."

The three other pilots watched in bewilderment as Lindy joined
them back in the sky. He signaled for each one to land, and one by
one they did as ordered. Then Lindy's plane came down again, this
time landing and stopping at the far end of the strip and away from

the rambunctious crowds. The officials quickly scrambled to greet him, dragging the stuffed mailbags in their wake. "The famous Lindbergh smile vanished and a frown accentuated with deep burrows in his brow came in its stead," a reporter from the *Journal* reported. Lindy, however, kept his cool and graciously accepted the city's regards. He never left the pilot's seat, and when all the mailbags were securely aboard, he left again, with the other planes in tow.

The ceremony was a bust for many in the crowd who patiently waited behind lines as directed. Even the luckiest spectators could see no more than Lindbergh's head bobbing just above the seat line of the aircraft. There was no wave or grand gesture to the crowd. That just wasn't Lindbergh's style. It was a disappointment, but the papers were kind enough: "Lindy, Modest as Ever, Evades Cheering Mob," the headlines read the next day.

In the air, Lindbergh was all business. He was, after all, back at his old job, a job that he would later admit was fraught with more danger day in and day out than making one singular yet monumental flight over the Atlantic. Rewards were personal ones on these missions: live to tell about it. Lindbergh and his hand-picked team flew the mailbags across the state, five round trips a week, trusting instincts and using only sight and occasionally a crude compass for navigation. On more subdued nights, under moonlit skies, there was time to think, possibly of greater achievements down the road. On other nights, it was a harrowing fight to survive. For Lindbergh, flying over Peoria again likely brought back memories.

One night in particular must have crossed his mind.

ON NOVEMBER 3, 1926, Lindbergh was soaring over the cornfields of Central Illinois when he hit a fog bank near Peoria. Expecting to land, the young pilot weighed his options. He flew in circles, hoping something, some brilliant idea, would pop into his head. It was 8 o'clock in the evening and while the weather certainly wasn't making matters any easier, Lindbergh discovered another, more insidious problem. His fuel was dangerously low. As it happened, a fueling mistake in St. Louis meant Lindbergh had drained the main tank of the refurbished Army de Havilland sooner than expected, and the reserve tank was just about tapped. An early November snow was falling, and visibility of ground lights was less than a half-mile. The Peoria airstrip was only faintly visible. "Twice I could see lights on the ground and descended to less than 200 feet before they disappeared from view," Lindbergh recalled.

With only minutes left in the reserve, he steered the craft east, hoping to find a clearing in the weather, but it was too late. At least he had made it to a less populated area. "I decided to leave the ship rather than land blindly." So he jumped.

Falling headfirst, he pulled on the ripcord and hoped for the best. Suddenly, the risers whipped around with a jerk and the free-falling weight at the bottom of the harness snapped back into an upright position. The chute was open. But a more precarious threat lay just below. Lindbergh placed the ripcord in his pocket and took out a flashlight. He pointed it downward. "The first indication that I was near ground was a gradual darkening of the space below," he recalled. Time was running out.

The snow had turned to a light rain, and the water-logged chute began to spin. It was too foggy to see but he could sense it: the ground was closing in. Then the chute stopped spinning just long enough to slow his descent. "I landed directly on a barbed wire fence without seeing it," he remembered.

Expecting the worst, he opened his eyes, surprised to be unharmed. The fence helped break the fall and the thick khaki aviation suit kept the barbs from penetrating his skin. He hadn't suffered a scratch. Lindbergh took his bundled parachute in hand and headed toward the nearest light. He found a road and followed it to a small town. From there, he would try to determine where he was and where his plane ended up. It was important he find the wreckage. Not because of the airplane, but because of the mail.

LONG BEFORE humans started flying mail across country, people were thinking about it. After all, when horseback, stagecoach, even bicycle were considered too slow in moving letters from town to town and state to state, the thought of delivering parcels using a machine of some type was being considered. When the rails were laid, the thought became a reality. Post offices were put on railcars. It was a marked improvement, but still not good enough. The locomotives provided more speed, but limited coverage. Then, in the mid-1800s, a British inventor named William Samuel Henson dreamed up a better plan. He applied for a patent to "transport letters, goods and passengers from place to place through the air." It was a wild notion. Henson knew powered flight was only a child's dream—there were no machines that could actually fly. But the idea was there. Nearly 50 years later, when the Wright brothers took flight, imagination soared. Flying the mail was no longer a pipe-dream but a possibility. Then it happened. After almost a decade of planning and government bickering, airmail was approved.

By then, flying was a business, albeit a risky one. Barnstormers or pilots doing daredevil stunts to entertain large crowds were scattered across the country. When the government sought pilots to fly letters across the country, there was no shortage of "crazy" men willing to do it.

Around the start of World War I, as European aircraft for the first time were making a slight dent in engagements overseas, many pilots left the stunt circuits and barnstorming tours and joined the newly minted U.S. Air Mail Service, not just for a steady job, but for army training too. At a little more than $80 a week, the money wasn't great, especially considering the risks involved. The pilots complained, but to little avail. The funds just weren't there, at least not yet, they were told. In the end, it didn't matter. They did it because they loved to fly.

In 1910, after heated debate, Congress had allocated about $50,-000 to start up an experimental operation, a trial run really, to see if flying the mail was feasible and cost-effective. On paper, it looked good. To prove the worth of delivering mail by air, they concluded, it was important that missions be completed on time, especially longer routes like Chicago to New York, which could save almost a full day in transit.

This would make airmail flights some of the most dangerous in the world, and the pilots who flew them, some of the bravest or craziest, depending on your point of view. The reasons were varied, but valid: there were only scattered designated landing sites; the planes were underpowered with temperamental engines; the planes had no brakes; their instruments were crude and unproven; and oftentimes good pilot instruction and intuition could be thrown out of whack if conditions suddenly changed.

The questionable quality of weather predictions was a major factor; low clouds and fog were the worst offenders in an unpredictable climate. With blind-landing technology using only instruments still many years away, pilots would improvise when caught in a sticky situation. Teaching such skills was primitive too. "After you cross the railroad tracks," one pilot would instruct another on flying through heavy fog, "pull up into the soup, count to thirty, then let down—that way you'll miss the high tension lines." The alternative, instructors warned, was obvious.

Skeptics wondered. How could pilots safely pull off these daily flights? The government, too, wanted to be sure.

In September of 1912, they got their first look, so to speak, when Earle Ovington, an American who trained in France, took a commissioned bag of letters and flew them six miles between post offices from Garden City, Long Island, to Mineola in a cramped, French-made monoplane named *Dragonfly*. The government granted permission for the stunt but was not yet ready to begin flying regular mail routes. This would be a good test. It was also a good show.

For a full week, once a day, Ovington made the round-trip flight, each time garnering more publicity for an aviation meet being held nearby. Ovington would fly over the post office building, circle several times, and wait as the postmaster nervously positioned himself below. Then, Ovington remembers, "I put the mail bag on my lap and worked the stick by putting my hands around it. I worked the bag, weighing 50 pounds, and let it go when I thought I would hit the postmaster." The postmaster looked up to see the large object falling toward his head. He ducked and quickly dashed out of the way. The results weren't always the same. "It would burst (on the ground) on more than one occasion," Ovington added. The crowds would clap and wave their hats in salute as the relieved postmaster gathered up the scattered letters. A government official was there to observe. Overall, he came away impressed but not fully convinced.

Six years later, with the backing of the armed services and a new military angle, airmail was ready to roll.

Earle Ovington in the monoplane *Dragonfly* testing airmail flight in Garden City, NY, 1912. Photograph courtesy the Library of Congress.

In May of 1918, the inaugural regular mail flight left the Polo Grounds in Washington, D.C. The war was still on and funds were low, but it was clear that military aviation had arrived. To secure a loftier Congressional allocation, the post office teamed with the National Advisory Committee for Aeronautics (NACA), an independent government body interested in promoting aviation. Air Mail routes, they argued, would not only be an invaluable service to the country but would also train young army pilots for cross-county flights. The army reluctantly got on board.

The papers were exalting in praise. "The free channels of the open air will be thrown open to the U.S. Mail," the *Washington Post* raved. But the post office was more cautious. It issued a press release that downplayed the significance of the event and emphasized the obvious: safety. "It is possible there may be some days where fog will interfere with the landing," the report conferred. It was an ominous early warning. Despite the risks, the mail was expected to arrive at its destination and on time. "It is not anticipated," the press release continued with some retribution, "that this will occur frequently, if at all."

The first flight was scheduled for an 11:30 AM takeoff time. Lieutenant George Boyle would be the pilot and Capt. Benjamin B. Lipsner, the first superintendent of the U.S. Air Mail Service, would oversee operations. Lipsner already had a sleepless night. A Chicago-born former automobile mechanic, Lipsner had switched to airplanes so he could work on engines in the army's aviation division. When Congress commissioned the army to run the first airmail service, Lipsner was put in charge of the fleet.

Boyle, the pilot, was another matter. Not the most experienced flyer in the lot (with fewer than 60 flight hours total), Boyle's fiancée just happened to be the daughter of Charles McChord, the Interstate Commerce Commissioner and a member of President Woodrow Wilson's cabinet. The President was expected to attend the launch.

The day had finally arrived. Lipsner took his position on the tarmac while Boyle readied the Jenny biplane. When the motorcade arrived, the President and Mrs. Wilson were warmly received. "He was being very careful of his bandaged hand," Lipsner recalled, as the President stepped from his vehicle. Several weeks before, during an armored car demonstration, Wilson touched a hot exhaust pipe and severally burnt his left hand. The President was still in some obvious discomfort and, apparent to Lipsner, in no mood for delays. "Mrs. Wilson stood beside him and showed a great deal of concern of his injured hand," Lipsner observed.

Greetings were cordial. Wilson handed Lipsner a signed letter addressed to the Postmaster of New York City. It was a ceremonial letter for charity. Once at its destination, the letter would be auctioned off in support of the Red Cross. The first bid of $1,000 was already in. The men posed for photos, then turned their attention to the plane.

"Contact," Boyle said from the cockpit as several men took hold of the propeller and gave it a spin.

Nothing happened. The propeller wouldn't go.

"Contact," Boyle said again. And still nothing.

Another try yielded a brief turn, cough, and puff of smoke, but the propeller only wiggled, then snapped back to a locked, upright position.

"What's the matter, Ben?" someone asked the superintendent, looking somewhat perplexed. Jennys were reliable planes that sometimes took a few turns to start, but this was worrisome.

"I don't know," Lipsner replied.

President Wilson, meanwhile, was getting antsy. He had a war to run and business elsewhere. He looked at his pocket watch, then turned to his wife and, as others heard him exclaim, said something like, "We are losing a lot of valuable time here." Lipsner knew it too.

Out of sheer desperation, Lipsner shouted, "Check the gas tank!" Sure enough, the tank was empty, a careless oversight. As soon as the tank was filled, the propeller was cocked again and this time caught a good spin. The plane roared down the dirt runway and into the clear blue sky, clearing the trees by three feet. The crowd roared. The first airmail bags were officially on their way. Lipsner breathed a little easier.

When the dust settled, President Wilson thanked the ground crew and waved to the crowd with his good hand before getting back in the car. At the same time, in a less harried event, an airmail pilot with another bag of letters had just taken off from New York's Belmont Park. Both flights would rendezvous in Philadelphia and exchange bags for a turnaround flight back to their respective cities. The plan, at least, was now literally up in the air.

Lipsner remembered looking up with pride as Boyle's plane climbed into the sky. Then he watched as it turned back around. Boyle had one last gesture before starting the trip. He turned back and buzzed over the airport, waving to the crowd below. Then up he went again. Lipsner, ever the worrywart on this day, took it all in. Then he tried to comprehend what his eyes were telling him. It just couldn't be, he thought to himself. He looked up again and this time was certain of it. Boyle was heading south.

Philadelphia was to the north.

"He's flying in the wrong direction," Lipsner muttered to himself.

Boyle's plane flew out of sight, dashing any hopes Lipsner had that the pilot would realize his mistake at some point and turn around. No one else, it seemed, had even noticed.

Lipsner waited anxiously in his office for the phone to ring, hoping to hear some good news. When the ring box finally chimed, Boyle was on the line. "Where are you?" Lipsner asked.

"My compass got a little mixed up," the pilot told him. Boyle said that he was in Waldorf, Maryland, about 25 miles south of Washington. "I landed in a cornfield," he explained, snapping a prop in the process.

President Woodrow Wilson and wife attending the inaugural airmail flight at the Polo Grounds in Washington D.C., May, 1918. Photograph courtesy Smithsonian National Post Office Museum Library.

Lipsner only had one question in response, one detail he could not ignore.

"What about the mail?" he asked.

THE DELAYED flight was an inauspicious beginning, but the rest of the day's activities were flawless and saved a lot of delivery time, just as the believers had hoped it would.

The day's success overall was also a good thing for the hapless Boyle. He was given another chance the next day. Flying in tandem with a second mail pilot who had to drop out halfway to Philadelphia with engine problems, Boyle kept on task and almost made it this time. But he overshot his target. Flying over the Atlantic and hopelessly lost, Boyle managed to find a spot of land and made a comical emergency landing at a country club, scaring the wits out of patrons below as the plane careened off the smooth grass, hit a fence, and broke a wing. Despite his obvious inexperience, postal officials asked to give the young pilot another chance, but within the ranks, the choice was clear. Boyle was reassigned.

In the first two years of airmail service, crashes were common and unavoidable, although in the first critical year, 1918, when the public's skepticism of the program was still running high, the ratio of fatalities to air miles, one for each 64,018 miles flown, was a statistic the superintendent of the airmail service at the time called "fantastic."

Still, the wrecks and forced landings frequently made the newspapers. Ed C. Randel, a mechanic who wrecked a plane on an experimental flight from Chicago to New York, was "pinned under the plane; gas tank fell on him," according to the report, but he was treated for an arm injury and released. Another pilot, Ed Gardner, a Midwestern boy from Plainfield, Illinois, broke his nose and blackened his eye; and M.A. Newton, flying over Belmont, New York, ran out of fuel and dropped the plane in a deep hole. It was so covered with dust and weeds, Newton explained through a broken and bandaged nose, that "it looked like solid ground from the air." Another pilot named Dean Smith crash-landed near a farmhouse. He walked away, but sent a telegram describing the wreck:

ON TRIP 4 WESTBOUND. FLYING LOW ENGINE QUIT. ONLY PLACE
TO LAND ON COW. KILLED COW.

Several flights were more tragic. The first fatality in 1918 was pilot Carl B. Smith near Elizabeth, New Jersey. The plane stalled and fell straight down, killing Smith instantly. Some claim that if Smith had been in the rear seat where the mail compartment was located, he might have survived. The back end of the aircraft saw little damage. "The mail," the final crash report concluded rather callously, "was saved."

By October of 1925, the government was issuing contracts for mail routes across the country, giving local aviation companies a chance for more business and profit. One such route was St. Louis to Chicago, officially listed as CAM-2, which would make scheduled stops in Springfield and Peoria before landing at a racetrack field in the Chicago suburb of Maywood.

The St. Louis-based Robertson Aircraft Company won the bid for CAM-2 and immediately started hiring pilots. Most of the men suited for the job were fresh out of the war and working barnstorming circuits for extra cash. Major Albert Lambert, who owned the airport and had a stake in the RAC, had a young pilot in mind to run the operations, an upstart barnstormer who was already living near Lambert Field and had a knack for thrill flying. His name was Charles Lindbergh. Lambert paid Lindy $200 a month to survey the routes and find good aviators to fly them. That spring, the first plane would go up. With more than 5,000 pieces of mail on board, the young pilot took off from St. Louis to Springfield to pick up another 15,000 letters. Then on to Peoria and finally Maywood, to drop the letters off for a transfer. The flight was flawless.

CAM-2 was always considered one of the most dangerous routes because of changing weather conditions. During summer months, daylight was abundant, but in the winter most flights would take off from St. Louis with darkness approaching. There were no directional lights on the plane or on the ground. The glow of a town would be the only visual reference. Fire pits were set at landing strips to guide the pilot's way, but if it was cloudy or overcast, navigation was nonexistent. In some cases, when sight indicators failed, it was better to just ditch a plane than try to fly it to the ground.

Unfortunately for the men running the CAM-2 route, this occurred several times.

On September 16, 1926, in a routine evening flight from Lambert Field, Lindbergh had just made a scheduled stop in Peoria and took off again when darkness fell and fog enveloped the plane. He turned back and attempted to drop a flare, but it did not ignite. He continued northeast and almost made it to Maywood, but he could not see a clear place to land. He headed back toward open fields and ditched the plane just as the gas tank went empty. His parachute opened, and he landed safely among the high stalks of the soon-to-be-harvested corn. The wreckage was found a few miles away, and the pilot took the mailbags, still intact, by hand to the nearby Ottawa post office for transfer to Chicago by train. Lindbergh's bravery and devotion to duty were enough for the Springfield postmaster to issue a proclamation: "We are all greatly rejoiced at the news of your safety which we watched for last night with great anxiety."

Less than six weeks later, near Peoria, Lindbergh was jumping out of his plane again for similar reasons.

This time, a barbed wire fence broke his parachuted fall.

IN A tiny rural community in central Illinois, B.K. (Pete) Thompson, a farmer, had just entered the small town's general store and was sitting down to a friendly game of cards when a "tall, slim man" walked in.

"Anyone hear a plane crash?" the stranger asked. He explained

TOP: Pete Thompson.

BOTTOM: Lindbergh's
wrecked plane in Covell, IL.

Photographs courtesy Rick
McDermott.

that he was looking for his wrecked plane and had no idea where
he was or where it went down. Thompson offered to help.

Together, the two men, both in their early 20s, climbed into the
farmer's Model T to search the country roads. "I'm an airmail pilot,"
the stranger told Thompson, and introduced himself as Charles
Lindbergh. Thompson told Lindbergh he was in Covell, Illinois,
about seven miles west of Bloomington. "I ran out of fuel over Peoria," Lindbergh explained.

The search for wreckage was fruitless; it was too dark. "Can you
give me a ride to the train station?" Lindbergh asked. The plan
was to take a train to Chicago and fly a new plane over the area

in the morning. The 10-mile drive on the dark, bumpy roads was treacherous and Lindbergh could hardly stand it. "For a man who had just ditched an airplane," Thompson recalled, "he sure held on for dear life."

If you find the wreckage, Lindbergh explained, there is a 38-caliber revolver in the cockpit.

"Guard the mail," he told Thompson.

Thompson found the wreckage the next day less than 500 feet south of his house. The plane's main landing gear had torn off at impact. The wings were completely gone, but the metal frame of the fuselage and tail were still intact. One wheel had broken loose and bounced a full hundred yards before crashing through a fence and resting—fully inflated—against the wall of a hog house.

The revolver was still there, right where the pilot had said it would be. And three large U.S. Air Mail bags were on board too—one was split open and slightly oiled, but still legible.

Around mid-morning, the whir of an engine was heard overhead. It was Lindbergh. He landed the reserve plane in a field next to the wreckage and was treated to a hearty fried chicken lunch "with all the trimmings" before loading up the airmail bags and heading back to Chicago to complete his route—some 24 hours late. But even the return trip was hampered by delays. "We spent about two hours trying to get the new plane started," Thompson recalls. "Lindbergh and I keep pulling the propeller, but it must have been too cold." Lindbergh had an idea. He went to the farmhouse and boiled 20 gallons of water to heat the radiator. "The engine kicked right over," Thompson said.

Thompson never saw the slim man again face-to-face, but he read about his heroics in the paper the following year. That's when he remembered what the young pilot had told him on the automobile trip to the train station that night. An idea Lindbergh had considered just months before on another mail run over Peoria. While flying placidly through the clouds, Lindbergh mused over the question of balancing weight, fuel, and distance and found an answer.

"It can be done and I'm thinking of trying it," he told Thompson.

Of course, he was talking about crossing the Atlantic.

One can only speculate, but perhaps the Illinois farmer was the first to hear those words spoken from a man who less than a calendar year later would be the most famous person in the world. Lindbergh would later say it was somewhere over Peoria, during another night run, where he started to wonder if he, or anyone for that matter, could fly nonstop over the ocean between hemispheres. It certainly wasn't an original idea; others had thought about it. A number of aviators had tried, without success. But they were doing it wrong, Lindbergh reasoned. It was pure physics, he thought. The right combination of weight distribution and fuel would be the only way to make it work.

For the next several months after ditching the plane in Covell, the flight across the ocean was all Lindy had on his mind. On moonlit nights, with no fog, he calculated the mechanics and risks in his head. He envisioned the heavy mailbags that crowded the cockpit as space and weight reserved only for fuel. He searched for every possible spot where weight could be reduced, including the padded seat on the airmail planes (he used a lighter wicker seat for the Atlantic flight).

When he secured backers, already lured by the coveted Orteig Prize, a challenge conceived by a wealthy French-born American named Raymond Orteig, Lindbergh put his ideas to work. Orteig, who owned several posh hotels in New York City, offered a $25,000 reward to anyone who could successfully fly an airplane nonstop from New York to Paris.

The *Spirit of St. Louis* was built to his specifications, and early on May 20, 1927, after an anxious Lindbergh was grounded several days by bad weather, the wheels of the single-engine plane finally lifted off the soggy runway at Roosevelt Field in New York and the "Flying Fool," as some hardened skeptics called him, was airborne. The next day, "Lucky Lindy" was in Paris.

"One thing for sure," author Winston Groom wrote in his book *The Aviators* about Lindbergh reaching the serene landscapes of Europe, "he was a long way from Peoria."

LESS THAN a year after the flight, as the adulations calmed down, Lindbergh took a job with a new aviation company called Transcontinental Air Company, as an ambassador of flight. He took a similar position with Pan American Airlines and also became a consultant for an aeronautical foundation, making close to a million a year with stocks and options thrown in. His accomplishments had finally paid off. Lindy was a wealthy man, and the air industry that he loved was becoming more than just a novelty, but an industry, led by its most popular figure, of course.

It was just after accepting the lucrative job offers and becoming financially secure for the first time in his life (he was even planning to marry soon) that Lindbergh was asked to fly the mail over Illinois one last time. He didn't have to do it, but said yes to help his friends.

"I am sorry I ran away from the crowd," Lindy said after touching down in Chicago a few hours after his scurried and rushed stop in Peoria. A similar crowd-control problem occurred in the Windy City when Lindy's plane was nearly mobbed and "a wing was almost torn to shreds," as a *Chicago Tribune* reporter noted.

"Lindy Gives Big Crowd the Slip," headlines blared, referring to the pilot's own words after the first leg of the flight was over. "I was nearly mobbed in Peoria so I gave the crowd the slip in Chicago to escape mishap," Lindbergh had said. "I wasn't trying to disappoint anyone, but it was evident when I came down here that another large crowd was waiting. Someone almost certainly would have gotten mitted up in the propeller."

With that, Lindy sneaked off to get some rest. He would do it all again in the morning, traveling the same route in the opposite direction. Crowds would be waiting for him again.

THE CELEBRATORY mail run for Lindbergh wasn't just for show. He genuinely cared about the future of aviation and especially supported his fellow pilots. Several years later, in a show of solidarity, he would have their backs again. In 1934, when President Franklin D. Roosevelt decided to cut costs and nationalize the mail routes by canceling airmail route contracts with civilian airlines and passing the job over to the U.S. Army, Lindbergh lashed out. He wrote a letter to the President, urging him to reconsider. Besides the obvious financial hit to carriers, it was a safety issue, Lindbergh insisted, arguing that inexperienced army pilots weren't equipped for such flights, especially at night. The results, Lindbergh and other aviation pioneers like World War I flying ace Eddie Rickenbacker claimed, would be disastrous and the aviation industry as a whole would be "unnecessarily damaged." The President wouldn't budge and issued the order without pause. In short time, just as Lindbergh and others had predicted, it happened: crashes, lots of them, occurred—and deaths too.

Only a few months after putting the army in charge, 66 planes went down and 10 serviceman pilots were killed, including three in one fateful day. Rickenbacker called it "legalized murder." Roosevelt, bowing to public pressure, reinstated private contractors with stipulations. The military was out of the airmail business.

Consequentially, the ill-conceived move and disastrous results had some benefit. It instituted a closer look at pilot training in general and eventually led to a federal investigation into why the Army's Air Service was in such disarray.

Lindbergh was behind it all, protecting an industry he loved. But the impasse with the president, while important, would be the least of his worries. A year later, the trial began against the man charged with kidnapping and killing Lindbergh's infant son in 1932. The night the world literally turned upside down for "Lucky Lindy."

In the early evening on the first of March, 20-month-old Charles Jr. was abducted while he slept in his bedroom crib. Two months later, the boy's badly decomposed body was found in a grove of trees near the Lindbergh home in East Amwell, New Jersey. Two years after that, an arrest was made. A man named Bruno Hauptmann was ultimately convicted.

Both Lindbergh and his wife Anne would testify at the trial, a highly publicized case thanks to the hero pilot's stature, but the tragic death of his first-born child and the hounding by the press was too much for a grieving Lindbergh. He was cold and distant toward reporters, a complacency that was exposed rather than respected. He never cried or showed any outward signs of emotion in public, an attitude his wife called "courageous," but others found crass and aloof. Everywhere he went the press followed and the coverage of the kidnapping, investigation and subsequent trial was a media circus. When it was over Lindbergh had had enough. He moved his family overseas.

Lindbergh's public persona took a major hit after the trial, and it would soon become controversial and downright ugly after moving abroad. While in Berlin for a tour, Lindbergh started to espouse his views on Germany, which he said was "strengthening (in a good way)" under Hitler's rule. Worse, for Americans, he felt the German nation was surpassing the United States in aviation, specifically military strength in the air. His apparent admiration for a fascist country run by a dictator was seen as insensitive, especially to the Jews. Lindbergh would eventually come back to the U.S. after the attack on Pearl Harbor and ask to be a part of the war effort, but his personal stance on war and Germany in general was too controversial. Officially, he was shut out of serving, but he tried to contribute as a test pilot in the South Pacific.

But that would come later. In 1928, at least for a brief period, America had a hero to cheer, and Lindbergh, before tragedy and controversies finally forced him into a sort of seclusion, seemed to accept the spotlight and adoring crowds.

His time as a mail pilot over Illinois would be part of his legend too. While not overlooked, it is often used to describe a young pilot who overcame the fears and obstacles of everyday flying to prepare for one glorious flight over the Atlantic. The crashes were one thing, but perseverance and commitment were another. Lindbergh, many agreed at the time, was an exemplary role model.

The final day he flew the mail to Peoria was another fine example. Lindbergh was all business, despite its showy purpose. And while concerns about crowd control and safety to his team understandably irked him and others, Lindbergh seemed to be happy back at his old post, back in the air, and in a place he was most comfortable: flying the mail and ready to jump out of the plane if needed.

AFTER A restful night in Chicago, Lindbergh and his team were set to go again in the morning. And as the papers noted, unlike the night before, "Lindy was in better spirits."

When Lindbergh touched down in Peoria on Tuesday, the crowds weren't as large, but they were just as excited. Hats waved in the air and children were held up high, bouncing on adults' shoulders, just to catch a glimpse of the hero pilot. Lindbergh obliged them with a wave and reporters even got a chance to question him.

"Just fine, it's a great life," he said when asked what it was like to be, well, Charles Lindbergh.

When someone asked if he was wearing a parachute on this flight, Lindy mulled the question over a bit. A parachute had saved his life several times while on the unpredictable mail routes, but it was something he did not bring along on the trip across the Atlantic. It weighed too much.

Lindy lifted the heavy pack off the ground.

"Of course, I'm an airmail pilot," he responded.

Before taking off again, Lindy posed for pictures. Then it was back to work. He waved to the crowd for the last time and dashed off to his plane.

"Oh boy, did you see that smile," one official remarked as the crowds cheered and Lindbergh, for the last time, took off down the Peoria runway to a brightening morning sky.

Within minutes, he was off the ground.

A MOTOR BUG'S DELIGHT

In March of 1896, Charles and Frank Duryea rolled out the first-ever commercial automobile. The Duryea Motor Wagon looked as strange as the sound it made. Ingeniously powered by a gasoline-fueled engine, it motored and sputtered slowly along. Hardly a time saver, that's for sure, but it was an ambitious venture. The Duryea brothers, a couple of bicycle makers from Canton, Illinois, had successfully created the first automobile-making business, based on designing, constructing, and selling the newfangled motor vehicles to the buying public. Being the first auto dealers also brought scrutiny. Not everyone was impressed or excited about the noisy contraptions. Less than three months later, in an "I told you so" moment, a New York City motorist in a Duryea Wagon struck a bicyclist. It was the nation's first traffic accident. The result was an embarrassment for the driver; he spent the night in jail. The bicyclist, for his part, suffered a broken leg. But the mishap did send a message that the automobile—not the bicycle, or horse for that matter—was the king of the road from now on. The car horn would soon follow. The next story is about automobiles, roads, and beautiful views. When the Peoria Park District was formed in 1893, the newly commissioned Parks Board set out to buy land and create public spaces that were not only scenic but easily accessible. The high bluff along the river on the north side of town was an ideal setting. But it was brutally steep and quite dangerous to traverse. The trolley car could access it from the top, but from the bottom, along the riverbank, the bluff was nearly impossible to reach. A path was needed so people could walk up. Plans were made, but it went slowly. By the time it was ready to build, nine years later, there were far more vehicles on the road. The winding path would have to be wide enough for automobiles too. Even its name was based on people using a "motor" rather than "foot" power to transport them up the side of the hill. It would be called a "drive," not a walkway. Theodore Roosevelt loved everything about the outdoors,

so it was no surprise that he was quite pleased when, during a visit to
Peoria, he was offered a chance to see the city in an open car. Roosevelt had just returned from a nearly yearlong trip to Europe and Africa where, in between big game hunts, he stewed over reports that his
handpicked successor for president, William Howard Taft, was wreck-
ing reform policies Roosevelt had fought so dearly to initiate and protect. While still deep in the African jungle, Roosevelt received a letter
that his friend, Gifford Pinchot, the longtime Secretary of Forestry,
was fired by Taft for speaking out against a corporate land grab in Alas-
ka orchestrated by the Taft Administration. That was enough for Roosevelt. He returned home and set out to embarrass Taft, fight for progressive ideals, support reform candidates in the midterm elections,
and, unbeknownst to him at the time, spearhead a movement support-
ing another run for the presidency. In October of 1910, thanks to an
invitation from an old friend, Roosevelt came to Peoria to fire up the
base. Fortunately for Peorians, politics wasn't the only thing on the
former president's agenda that day. He also took a car ride up the hill.

THEODORE ROOSEVELT stepped off the train in Peoria, Illinois,
around 1:30 PM on October 12, 1910: Columbus Day. The jovial ex-
president wasted no time, as usual. He adjusted his black fedora
hat, buttoned his overcoat, and stormed toward a "feeble-looking"
man who had taken a seat in the corner of the station, just beyond
the crush of the well-wishers said to number in the hundreds. Roosevelt charged like a bull toward the man as the throng erupted.
"As soon as Mr. Roosevelt saw the archbishop he broke through the
lines and greeted the venerable churchman," the *New-York Tribune*
exulted, "a movement which almost led to a riot."

   "The greeting was a simple, but a fervent handshake," the *Peoria Journal* explained. "Colonel Roosevelt seemed in his element...
nodding and smiling...the omnipresent glasses were there and the
gleaming teeth seemed to emphasis 'De-e-e-lighted.' Cheers after
cheers....yell after yell...and through it all the colonel smiled and
enjoyed it."

   Archbishop John L. Spalding was just as enthralled. Although a
stroke in 1905 led to an early retirement for the patriarch of Peoria
Catholic schools, Spalding was still an influential and inspirational

TOP: Archbishop John L. Spalding.

RIGHT: Theodore Roosevelt.

Photographs courtesy the Library of Congress.

figure. "One of the very best men to be found in the entire country," Roosevelt would later write about Spalding in his autobiography.

Spalding had asked Roosevelt to make a full stop in Peoria and join him for lunch and, later that evening, a speaking event at the local Knights of Columbus Hall. Roosevelt graciously accepted and told Spalding he would use the occasion to also honor the retired archbishop.

Now Roosevelt took Spalding by the arm and, as "the people broke all lines and strove to get to the ex-president," the two estimable men walked to a waiting automobile.

"The colonel was up bright and early and experienced not the

Theodore Roosevelt and pilot Archibald Hoxsey at Kinloch Field, St. Louis, October 11, 1910. Photograph courtesy the Library of Congress.

slightest effects from his extremely strenuous visit to St. Louis," the papers noted.

Strenuous, yes, but thrilling too!

Just the day before, Roosevelt had visited St. Louis' Kinloch Field as the distinguished guest of an airshow exhibition featuring the Wright Brothers aviation team. At the airstrip, a skinny young aviator named Archibald Hoxsey had approached Roosevelt to tell the former president that they shared the same birth date, October 27. Hoxsey may have been kidding. His birth date is listed in many instances as October 15. But it didn't matter.

"He smiled," Hoxsey recalled, "and I knew I had him."

Hoxsey was Roosevelt's kind of guy: an adventurer, exhibitionist, and daredevil all rolled into one. The Wright Brothers hired him for his spunk, but Hoxsey soon became a bit of a liability. Once, he drew the ire of the Wrights, who warned their young aviator not to take so many "unnecessary risks." But Hoxsey could not be held down. He wanted to fly longer and soar higher each time he stepped into the plane. Damn the odds.

It was the kind of moxie Roosevelt admired.

In a speech given just months before meeting the upstart flyer, Roosevelt defended any man who took on critics and doubters and bravely succeeded, regardless the outcome:

"The credit belongs to the man who is actually in the arena, whose face is marred by dust and sweat and blood; who strives valiantly; who errs; who comes short again and again because there is no effort without error and shortcoming; but who does actually strive to do the deeds, who knows great enthusiasms, the great devotions; who spends himself in a worthy cause; who at the best knows in the end the triumph of high achievement, and who at the worst, if he fails at least fails while daring greatly, so that his place shall never be with those cold or timid souls who neither know victory nor defeat."

Hoxsey was born in Staunton, Illinois, and took to piloting like a prizefighter to a match, always pushing the limits of his own ability and that of the British-made biplane, designed by Howard T. Wright (no relation to the Kitty Hawk brothers). Used for longer flights, the biplane looked like a transparent bird with two parallel booms in front and four in back. The engine sat directly behind the two open-aired seats, and the two main wings, both 36 feet in length, were above and below the cockpit. A rudder and smaller tail wing off the back boom would scrape the ground. It looked light, flimsy, and clumsy standing still, but it soared like an eagle in flight.

Hoxsey was already making national headlines. He became the first man to fly a plane at night and, a day before Roosevelt's visit to St. Louis, broke the sustained flight record of 104 miles, a trip that originated in Springfield, Illinois, and covered a distance that Hoxsey estimated on his own.

When Hoxsey arrived at Kinloch that day, spectators at the airstrip shaded their eyes and wondered why the plane kept flying overhead for an extra 57 minutes, sputtering in circles and drifting hopelessly off course then back again. It was a hazy day, and Hoxsey says he mistook the smoke from a nearby brick factory for the tar-pit marker on the field. He eventually landed at a country club three miles south of the strip, but finally back on land.

The next day, he met the former president.

"I envy you," Roosevelt told the pilot, shaking his hand.

"Then here is your chance to fly with me," Hoxsey said.

"No," Roosevelt replied, somewhat surprised by the offer.

"You can trust me," Hoxsey retorted convincingly. "We have the same birthday."

Roosevelt couldn't wait. He removed his jacket and dashed for the plane.

Missouri Governor Herbert Hadley was standing nearby. "Are you really going up?" he shouted.

"Of course I am," the colonel said excitedly.

Hoxsey, however, was having second thoughts. "I keep telling myself, now Hoxsey, no funny business when you get this fellow up because if you spill him you can never square yourself with anybody."

No worries. The flight was flawless, and Roosevelt was giddy, "waving his hat to the crowd" as the plane dived low and swept past the pavilion seats.

"Don't pull any of them strings," Hoxsey said, shouting over the incessant whine of the engine and referring to the valve cord directly over Roosevelt's head, which, if pulled, would have stopped the engine cold. The colonel smiled back that "toothy grin," Hoxsey remembered. "Nothing doing," the ex-president shouted back.

Surprisingly, for a man who just a year earlier had hunted down, shot, killed, and collected "for science" an elephant, giraffe, lion, and rhinoceros during an expedition in East Africa, the plane ride, Roosevelt's first, made for "the most exciting day of my life," he declared.

It was somewhat less amusing for the Wright Brothers, who later chastised Hoxsey for the heedless stunt, which could have ruined them if it had gone wrong. They scolded the hotshot pilot in private and nearly fired him on the spot. But the celebrated ride was a rousing success, and the story of "Teddy's first flight" made headlines in just about every newspaper in the country. Archibald Hoxsey, the 26-year-old wunderkind pilot, became an instant celebrity.

Less than three months later, he was dead.

On December 30, while trying to break his own altitude record of nearly 12,000 feet, Hoxsey flew straight into a gusty crosswind, lost control, and spun wildly back to Earth. "He used a mighty effort to right himself," a colleague explained, "right up to the last second of his life." Just before striking the ground, the plane somersaulted. Those who witnessed the impact thought Hoxsey might have survived the crash. But upon arriving at the wreck site, they found his lifeless body gored by the jagged end of an iron bar from the transmission assembly. The Wright Brothers graciously offered to pay for the funeral.

IN PEORIA, Roosevelt and Archbishop Spalding left the train station and, along with several other local dignitaries, hopped in Peoria-made Glide automobiles for a trip through the city and a late lunch at the lavish Peoria Country Club on the bluff overlooking the Illinois River. The crowds were waiting along the route. "From the National Hotel until he passed through the confines of the village of Averyville," the papers reported, "Col. Roosevelt's progress was one continued ovation."

The vehicles were nearly obscured by a group of bicyclists who rode alongside and in the motorcade's wake. The procession made its way past the Avery plant, where workers cheered "wild huzzas for Teddy."

"That's the kind of cheering I like to hear," the colonel chortled. "It's spontaneous. It comes from the heart."

At Kingman School on Adams Street, Roosevelt was moved by the numbers of children lining the curb sides, waving flags. He stood up, smiled, and waved back. "At this juncture," the papers noted, "an unlooked-for interruption occurred." A teacher named Phelps ran out into the street directly in front of the vehicle and unfurled a huge American flag. The driver hit the brakes just in time. Roosevelt couldn't help himself. He opened the car door and jumped out, giving Phelps a firm handshake and patting each child on the head. "A hundred little hands were reaching for the colonel in every direction and they swarmed around him like flies," the *Evening Star* wrote. The occupants of the car in the rear of the procession stood up to see what all the commotion was about and cheered when they realized it was "Teddy" greeting the children in the street. After ten minutes, Roosevelt was back in the vehicle and to "a shrill treble of childish good-byes," the paper reported, the motorcade was off again.

There were no speeches planned at the luncheon, the papers explained, in anticipation of Roosevelt's words that night at the auditorium. But the car ride to the country club was something special indeed. Roosevelt settled in the Glide as it picked up speed and headed north out of downtown.

Like the former president, the Glide was a workhorse. Similar in size and comfort to the popular Packard, both vehicles were considered touring machines, which meant they were slightly larger than most vehicles on the road and designed for longer, more sustained trips, rather than short jaunts in the city. Made by the Bartholomew Company in Peoria Heights, whose huge headquarters and plant sat on the high side bluff, the Glide was a first-rate "Hill Climber, Built in the Hills," the ads announced. The Model G Special featured a rear bench seat that was raised to give passengers in the back a better view. "Ride a Glide, Then Decide" was the company's slogan.

Although it was good theater, especially for the reporters, the brief interludes along the route were wasting precious time. No more stops, the colonel was told as they proceeded to the country club for lunch. They were already running late. But the procession would be interrupted again.

The entourage of Glides made a left turn off North Adams Street, which ran parallel to the Illinois River in an area known as the narrows due to the river's narrow channel between a tree-lined gorge and the rocky wall of the bluff. A road just below the bluff hugged the river on one side and the wall on the other. Roosevelt must have thought he was leaving the striking view of the river behind at the shoreline, but as the gravel road gradually snaked its way up the hillside, he soon found out that was not the case.

As others already knew, Roosevelt was in for a special treat.

SEVEN YEARS earlier, in October of 1903, members of the Peoria Parks Board and the board president at the time, a man named Benjamin Warren Jr., gathered for a modest but important ceremony at the very site where Roosevelt's entourage would turn off on North Adams. Warren was handed a "new" shovel, said a few brief words, smiled, then drove the blade into the ground and turned over the dirt. With that, the building of an ambitious new public road was underway.

Theodore Roosevelt in a
Glide on Adams Street in
Peoria, October 12, 1910.
Archbishop Spalding is
seated next to Roosevelt
in the black fedora. Photo-
graphs courtesy the Wheels
O' Time Museum, Dunlap,
IL, and the Local History
and Genealogy Collection,
Peoria Public Library, Peo-
ria, IL.

The idea of a road up the hill and around the brow of the bluffs
actually began in 1893 when the state of Illinois passed legislation
called the Pleasure Driveway and Parks District Act, giving individual cities the power to vote and act on beautifying and fortify-
ing some of the state's natural resources. In essence, the state was
making a suggestion to the cities: build more public parks.

In Peoria, the choice was clear. The high bluff on the north side
of town was easily the most scenic, but it was privately owned and
inaccessible. The newly formed Parks Board sought to change that.
They asked private owners to donate or sell parcels, which some
did. But finances were tight. There wasn't enough money to buy

all the land and build a park, so the plan would have to wait. The already purchased property was placed in escrow.

Nine years later, in 1902, with more money in hand, the park idea was on again. The renowned engineer and architect Oscar F. Dubois was hired to map a 2.5-mile route from the bottom of the bluff to the high point known as Prospect Heights. Dubois, who was already known locally for designing Glen Oak Park and Laura Bradley Park, had a vision that included preserving as much of the area's natural landscape as possible, especially the majestic red and white oak, pine, and maple trees that gave the bluff its character and color, especially in the fall. Instead of connecting with Madison Street, which was the original plan, Dubois suggested an additional 100-foot right-of-way to Adams Street. In that way he assured an unobstructed view of the river. The proposed "driveway" was adopted by resolution in November, 1902, and the city started to buy up the rest of the land. The largest plot, nearly 24,000 acres, was purchased from a H.F. Darwin for $4,037, records show. Even some businesses, such as the Brick & Tile Co. and Peoria Water Works, had land on the proposed trail. When all the necessary legal details were settled and papers signed, ordinances were passed that guaranteed the tracts would be used for one purpose only: as a recreational street to be enjoyed by all. On October 14, 1903, at 2:30 PM, after Warren's shovel pierced the ground and the rest of the Parks Board members cheered in approval, work began in earnest.

It took three months, a team of horses for "grading and grubbing," and a gaggle of hired laborers with picks and shovels to remove the dense undergrowth and clear the way. In December, the 30-foot-wide path was graveled eight inches deep. Now it looked more like a road. The vision had become reality. Even the city officials who signed the purchase papers were impressed. When it came time to name the new roadway, one suggestion seemed to rise above all others—a reflection of the beautiful scenery now accessible by motor vehicle and shared by all. The vote was unanimous.

The new roadway would be called Grand View Drive.

ROOSEVELT AND the archbishop sat in the back of the Glide as it made its way up Grand View Drive to the top of the vista. At some point, Roosevelt motioned for the driver to stop. Once the car was safely idle, Roosevelt stood up from his back-seat perch and stared at the sweeping view of the Illinois River below, stretching out in both directions like a winding rope; the blue sky reflecting from the expanse of smooth water. The tops of the tree-covered bluffs were a palette of spectacular fall colors.

To understand exactly what Roosevelt viewed that day is best left to those who recorded for history's sake the beauty of Prospect Hill. Rising nearly 1,000 feet above the river, it had "the most extended and charming landscape views in the west." This lucid description is found in the *History of Peoria,* a book written before the turn of the 20th century:

The upper end of Lake Peoria (the widest part of the Illinois River), some fifteen miles away, is plainly visible, as are the city of Chillicothe still beyond and the villages of Rome and Mossville along its border. When the atmosphere is very clear the city of Lacon, on the opposite side of the river, twenty-five miles distance can be seen. The country beyond presents a greatly undulating surface of fertile prairie and woodland, which is converted into finely improved farms of rare productiveness.

Of course, the centerpiece of the view was the Illinois River.

Roosevelt stopped and soaked it all in.

"Great! That's fine," he said out loud, and told the archbishop that it reminded him of the view from his home on Sagamore Hill overlooking Oyster Bay in Long Island, New York.

A newspaper reporter recorded the moment, gushing praise upon the breathtaking scenery and Roosevelt's reaction: "As each new vista unfolded itself the colonel grew more empathic in his admiration, which had not abated by the time he reached the Country Club."

And that was it.

The papers didn't add much more.

Later, Roosevelt would be credited with a phrase that still resonates with Peorians today. Recalling the trip on the bluff, he purportedly claimed it to be "the world's most beautiful drive."

The World's Most Beautiful Drive!

Imagine that.

WHERE AND when Roosevelt actually said those words is debatable. One report has the former president making the comment on the way back down from the country club. Perhaps seeing the view again, Roosevelt was moved to respond when one of the hosts supposedly apologized for the rough roads. As the story goes, the colonel replied, "What difference does it make? I have traveled all over the world, and this is the world's most beautiful drive."

It's important to note that Roosevelt's words, if spoken as written, were as much an endorsement of where he was and what he was doing as they were an affirmation of the spectacular scenery before him. After all, he did say it was the most beautiful "drive," not necessarily the most beautiful "view."

The view *was* stunning, of course, and everyone agreed. But there were other reasons the colonel was impressed that day.

For one, he was in an automobile.

At the time, motored vehicles, even workhorses like the Glide, were limited in where they could go. Some streets were being paved with graveled rocks topped by a layer of coal, a modest improvement over cobblestones, but most roads were dusty dirt paths, and few went to remote places. Roosevelt had seen some beautiful sites in his life but mostly on foot, by boat or on horseback. Seeing the nation's natural wonders from the back of an automobile was an entirely new concept for the colonel, like flying in an airplane.

He captured the moment like a photograph.

THIS CONCEPT of stretching the limits of travel by automobile, however, wasn't entirely new. Times were changing, and drivers were bent on breaking barriers, especially when it came to the virgin machines. Faster speeds and longer trips were some of the sporty highlights. Cross-country ventures—literally, crossing the country— were gaining momentum, although few had actually accomplished it. The newfangled motor vehicles were simply too unpredictable and unproven, and roads were too unreliable. The vehicles certainly weren't built to go over mountains, traverse rivers, and survive the desert-like heat and dust of the open plains. In some places, there wasn't even a path, let alone a road to follow. But that didn't stop a few brave go-getters from giving it a try.

John and Louise Davis set off from New York in a Duryea, 1899. Photograph courtesy *Scientific American*.

Even families got into the act.

In 1899, the first transcontinental crossing by an automobile was attempted by a New York couple, John and Louise Davis. It may be that the idea was a publicity stunt conjured up by the car's manufacturer to prove the worth of American vehicles over European counterparts, which was an acceptable challenge at the time. But Mr. Davis insisted otherwise, claiming his doctor hatched the idea by recommending that he "stay out of doors for a year" and end up in a healthier and less polluted area like, say, San Francisco.

It's not as if the two socialites weren't qualified to take on such a grand venture. John was a mechanic by trade, although almost everyone was an inexperienced driver. And Louise was a journalist. Her resume included *The New Haven Palladium*, among many other New York area newspapers. As many as six magazines contacted her to write about the trip.

On July 13, at the corner of Broadway and 35TH in downtown Manhattan, the Davises set off in their recently built Duryea, a flimsy motor coach with a two-cylinder engine that puttered along comfortably at 10 miles an hour but was able to reach the daredevil speed, the manufacturer overhyped, of 35 MPH in third, or high gear. The Duryea machine had roots in Central Illinois, thanks to two brothers, Frank and Charles Duryea, who grew up near Canton, Illinois, and built bicycles, then motor vehicles, and produced the first gasoline-powered automobile in Springfield, Massachusetts.

Charles would eventually bring the business back to Illinois and for a time manufactured a Duryea model in Peoria.

The Duryea was basically a horse buggy with an engine in the back. On the right side of the driver was a lever used for steering and on the left were two levers controlling the brakes. The gas tank was located directly behind the single bench seat. It was a glorified carriage, many felt, and so painfully slow that the only thing that could give it a boost, critics quipped, would be the four-legged component conspicuously missing up front.

"Where's the horse?" they asked.

The Davises set off to joyful shouts from "a thousand throats" and proceeded to motor carefully through the crowds, taking nearly an hour just to reach the Hudson River. "This is to Frisco or bust!" Davis enthusiastically shouted as they left their cheering friends in the dust. Three grueling months later, in October, the Davises reached Chicago, just under halfway. The trip was effectively over.

Hampered by breakdowns and embarrassing delays, including a court-ordered three-week stoppage in Toledo so a claim warrant could be heard against the Duryea's manufacturer, the Davises' vehicle limped into the Windy City bruised and battered. The couple vowed to continue their journey with a new rear axle—which had broken for the second time—but no records show them continuing west of Chicago. Perhaps the most humiliating episode occurred only weeks into the trip, when a one-armed bicyclist named Albert Roe left New York City ten days after the Davises. Roe claimed he could cross the continent on a two-wheeler going 60-75 miles a day. In Syracuse, New York, after only five days, Roe pedaled past the creeping Duryea.

The trip was considered "a bust" by the motor vehicle industry announcing its "immediate termination," and sparing any additional embarrassment. The *Scientific American*, normally a trade sheet that supported such inventions, reported that "trips of this nature did more harm than good to the industry."

One thing was painfully clear: if such an adventure was to be attempted again, motor vehicles would need to be more durable and roads would have to be improved.

The car builders took up the challenge. The next attempt was by automaker Alexander Winton in his own Winton touring car in 1903. Winton was accompanied by another man, an observer really, Charles Shanks, who dispatched reports from the road to the *Cleveland Plain Dealer* (the sponsor of the trip). The two men decided to go in the opposite direction—from San Francisco to New York—tackling the challenging mountains first. They immediately took a wrong turn but eventually made it to the Sierras. It was all downhill from there. A wheel fell off a rocky plateau, the car was stranded by snow in Summit, California, and Mill City, Nevada, and they became hopelessly stuck in the soft sand of the desert plains. Mercifully, that was the end. Winton gave up with only 530 miles logged and nine days on the road. The two men walked to the nearest depot, boarded a train back home to Cleveland, and left the car stranded in its sandy grave. "The trip is off," the *Plain Dealer* reported, and then, adding insult to injury, declared, "The adventurous tourists will finish their trip in a Pullman car."

The following year, Dr. H. Nelson Jackson, a Vermont surgeon, and a handy mechanic named Sewall Crocker boarded another Winton and completed a reported "6,000-mile journey" from San Francisco to New York in 63 days, 12 hours, and 30 minutes. The total mileage alone should have raised some eyebrows. The actual cross-country distance, from sea to shining sea, in a relativity straight line, is just short of 3,000 miles. "Old mileages are not the same as new mileages," writes auto historian Curt McConnell, describing the obvious discrepancy. "Early roads often zigzagged along section lines." But a journey of that distance had some explaining to do.

In stretches out west, in mountainous terrain, it was anybody's guess where the two men went and how they got there. The stories dispatched were a mix of embellishment, imagination, and speculation, fueled by the drivers themselves who refused to talk to reporters until they reached the flatter plains of the Midwest. They would have made it several weeks sooner, they boasted, but sat idle for 19 days total in California, Idaho and Wyoming, waiting for parts. Nevertheless, the first transcontinental trip by automobile was completed. That no one could dispute. And a new record was established that others were chomping at the bit to break.

That same year, three men in a Packard would complete the same route, but at a shorter distance of 4,000 miles, again speculative, in 62 days. Four more successful attempts would take place over the next three years.

Then, in 1906, two families decided to give it a try—in a Glide.

On June 7, William S. Gehr of Wenatchee, Washington, his wife, Emma, and their dog, Snip, along with friends William Edward Camfield, wife Nellie, and 8-year-old son William Jr., boarded a Model E Glide for a cross-country jaunt from Wenatchee, about a hundred miles east of Seattle to New York City. "This is not a speed record," Mr. Gehr proclaimed. "It's a recreation trip." But as the papers quickly noted, it was the first transcontinental attempt that included several women, a child, and a family pet.

Mr. Gehr was right on. The family had no intention of making any time constraints. They casually made their way across country, camping, fishing, hunting, and generally enjoying the great outdoors. If there was a breakdown, they would stop and enjoy the apparent respite, oftentimes staying put for several days just for rest and relaxation. Eventually, the papers caught on. This was no race; this was a vacation—the first family road trip.

On October 13, after spending nearly four full months on the road, the two families rolled into Peoria, Illinois, "tanned to a ripe berry color and with clothes and features coated with Illinois dust," the *Peoria Herald-Transcript* reported.

Illinois was certainly on the route, but Peoria was special for another reason. It was home to the Glide. Peanut roaster turned car maker, Jay Bartholomew didn't let the opportunity slip by. He formally greeted the families in Princeville and escorted them to Peoria. "The travel-worn machine demonstrated its friskiness in covering the twenty-five miles to Peoria in a trifle over an hour," the papers praised. When they arrived in front of the Bartholomew Glide factory, they were greeted by a large crowd and a rousing applause.

"A spade projected from the pile of baggage on the back of the machine, a tire worn until the canvas projected in a fringe; a deep dent in the radiator screen made by a forest stump, and a water line near the top of the tonneau...told some of the trials endured by the travelers."

Mr. Gehr was an animated interview. While traveling in South Dakota, he told reporters, torrential downpours turned the road into an impossible "morass of gumbo." They waited in the comfort of hotels until the weather cleared. Before that, in Yellowstone, a bear snatched their morning bacon. "The only adventure with wild animals," Gehr explained. And in Montana, a group of Indians near the Flathead River laughed at their predicaments at first but eventually used their saddle horses to extricate the vehicle's wheels from a deep hole. Then a farmer lent them a cowhide to patch a flat.

In Iowa, Gehr concluded, the travel was "fine," hampered only by a stiff wind in Davenport that caused a brief delay.

Despite their weariness, the two families were clearly in good spirits. "We have enjoyed the trip immensely," said Mrs. Gehr. "The hardships were only part of the journey and we enjoyed them as they came." Even Gehr's "handsome" Pointer, Snip, got a mention: "She [Snip] rode the entire trip in the front of the auto, acting as guard at night and made herself useful generally…proud of her position as if she was a full licensed chauffeur."

The families were expected to stay in Peoria only a few days, but that turned into a full week before they set off again. The ambitious plan was to go to New York and complete the west-to-east journey, then travel to Washington, D.C., and south to Florida. Later, they would go to Mexico, taking their leisurely time along the way. But Bartholomew had other ideas for his now nationally recognized endurance machine.

A large auto tradeshow was coming up in New York City, and Bartholomew wanted the Gehrs' Glide to be a prominent feature. Whether the rich entrepreneur paid the families or just used his power of persuasion is not known. The Gehrs apparently agreed to the proposal, although it clearly meant big changes in their schedule. Now they had a deadline to meet. The big auto show was in December. For the first time in their long journey, the Gehrs were in a hurry.

On November 23, the two families drove into Linesville, Pennsylvania, an impressive feat for sure, but still some 400 miles from their destination. Just five days later, on the 28th, the Glide made it to New York City, but the Gehrs were not in it. For reasons only

The Gehrs and Camfields with dog Snip, and the Glide, somewhere in the middle of their cross-country trip from Wenatchee, WA, to New York, 1906. Photograph courtesy the Wheels O' Time Museum, Dunlap, IL.

explained by their obvious intent to get the vehicle to New York City within days, the roadster was loaded onto a railcar and shipped to the Big Apple instead. The Grand Central Palace Auto Show opened on December 1. They never would have made it on time. When the Glide arrived in New York City, Bartholomew never let on. He had his showcase vehicle on display and the Gehrs bold American road trip was over. Even the *New York Times* was duped. "While automobiles have previously crossed the continent," the paper gushed, "this is the first time that the journey had been successfully accomplished by a regular touring car carrying its full compliments." The paper also pointed out that it was the first time the journey had been completed with a female passenger on board, two in fact, or three if you count the dog. Later, Emma Gehr's journal would confirm any suspicions. They never made it all the way to New York, she stated, which would have truly constituted a transcontinental trip.

Two years later, in 1908, another family, the Murdocks, took a Packard stuffed with seven people, including four children, and successfully made the California-to-New York route in 32 days, 3 hours, and 7 minutes. Upon completion, Frank Murdock, the patriarch, predicted "cross-country road trips would scarcely get a mention" in the coming years. But he was wrong.

Although the floodgates were opened thanks to the Murdocks and Gehrs, many roads were still impassable or not built at all. So adventure trips by automobile were still considered risky, mostly a novelty, but they were popular in the public consciousness. In 1910, when Roosevelt came to Peoria and rode a Glide, the newspapers that summer were filled with stories of no fewer than six vehicles attempting transcontinental trips. Roosevelt, being quite the explorer himself, was likely thrilled by them all.

Now, in Peoria, the former president was thoroughly enjoying his own road adventure, holding tightly onto the side of the Glide and flashing his "toothy grin" as it motored up the side of the hilly, windy path, hitting bumps and ruts along the way.

"Stop!" Roosevelt cried at several points, just to admire the view.

AFTER LUNCH at the country club on the bluff and the return trip back down Grand View Drive, the next stop was the archbishop's lavish residence on Glen Oak Avenue. A crowd was waiting for the former president. Roosevelt welcomed all who came to greet him. "Men and women, old men and women; the school girl and boy, boys and girls in arms, all passed by and were given a cordial hand shake and smile," the *Herald-Transcript* reported. Roosevelt was delighted to see a boy, only eight years old, the papers described, who held his five-year-old brother in his arms. "That boy's alright," said a smiling Roosevelt. "That's fine of you bubby. When a brother will carry his little brother around that way, that boy will make a good citizen." When a farmer walked up to the ex-president with a "bullwhip" in his hand, Roosevelt laughed.

That evening, when the car rides and ceremonial greetings were over, Roosevelt got down to business. He was, after all, on an important mission. At the Knights of Columbus Hall, referred to as "the coliseum" in the papers, a packed audience witnessed a more subdued and serious Roosevelt use the pulpit to wage battle against corrupt politicians.

Roosevelt had lost none of his vigor as a public speaker and now had a worthy cause. The 52-year-old was reluctantly returning to politics nearly two years after deciding not to run for another full term as president. Roosevelt's chosen successor and one-time ally, William Howard Taft, had betrayed past policies and corruption was rampant, in the ex-president's mind.

Roosevelt vowed not to seek a second full term as president, a choice afforded to him by inheriting the Oval Office after McKinley's assassination, but he was strongly against Taft. If Taft was renominated as the Republican candidate for the 1912 election, many wondered, might "Teddy" change his mind and run against his old friend? That decision would come later. Roosevelt's train-stop tour through the Heartland was a grassroots effort to garner support against corrupt individuals or, as Roosevelt called them, "jack potters": politicians who hit the jackpot by using their authority and power for personal and financial gain. The crowds were large, the papers noted, and excited to hear the ex-president speak. "Take down the 'jack potters,' " many shouted.

"If a man is a crook," Roosevelt told them, "hunt him out of public life. If you don't, you are harming this country not only for yourselves but for your children and your children's children." He asked for an army to join him.

"But it rests, my friends, with you, to do it in Illinois," he continued. "I can disagree with honorable men on public questions. I can fight hard for my side and if I win, I'm glad and if I don't win, I am sorry. And I can submit to it. But when it is a question of corruption, I recognize no party lines."

Roosevelt was due in Indianapolis the next day and, after the speech, went immediately to his train. As for his day in Peoria, the *Washington D.C. Times* summed it up this way: "Compared with yesterday in St. Louis, with its wild auto dashes, the colonel's airship flight, and dozens of speeches, this was a comparatively quiet day."

The people of Peoria view it much differently, however. Roosevelt's visit would forever honor a city. "I shall take a moment to tell you, my good people, how much I admire your town and your river. I like all of your products. But I like the citizens the best," he said.

Strong words of praise from a respected statesman like Roosevelt.

But it's what he said about the road on the hill that Peorians remember best.

THE GLIDE made it only until the early 1920s. Having trouble competing with the Cadillacs, Oldsmobiles, and Fords, Bartholomew merged with the Avery Company to try and save his automobile.

But the truck and tractor manufacturer filed for bankruptcy and went into receivership in 1923. The Glide was history.

As roads improved, so did travel. By the 1920s, automobiles had become sturdier and stronger, and speed demons in sporty road-sters were making the cross-country trip in less than two weeks, instead of months. The public interest, however, ended. Although transcontinental ventures were still occurring after World War I, automobiles could now make a coast-to-coast trip with only a hand-ful of stops for gas. Where's the danger? No longer were a few brave pioneers risking their lives just for adventure. Thanks to the Gehrs, though, Peoria has its place within its lore. By the 1960s, once the interstates were beginning to criss-cross the nation, the family road trip would become a staple of American culture.

Grand View Drive was eventually paved when technology finally allowed, but it would be some 30 years after Roosevelt's visit. Gravel country roads were the norm in the early half of the 20TH century and best attempts were being made to keep them up. "The rapidly increasing use by automobiles of our driveways and boulevards has made their maintenance and the dust nuisance a problem," the city of Peoria reported in a 1915 annual review. "Sprinkling has been quite an item on account of the protracted droughts."

Still, the city had no problem touting itself in tourism ads as "The Mecca of the Automobilist." And for its scenic drives through beautiful parks: "A Motor Bug's Delight." The road on the hill was a fine example.

There are few more charming landscapes on earth than that which greet your eyes from these high bluffs. The view is rare because of the unusual combination of hill and forest, with pas-ture, meadow and fields of growing grain, far below in the valley through which winds the placid and silvery Illinois. The many colors of the growing crops blending with the trees the river and sky, make a scene that is rare to find.

It is interesting that Roosevelt's quote is not included in the early ads. In fact, his supposed five famous words did not appear in print until much later, years after his visit. In another ironic spin, there's the question of whether or not Peoria's powerhouse AM radio station and one of its oldest, WMBD, used Roosevelt's words as an acronym

Grand View Drive, 1910. Photograph courtesy the Local History and Genealogy Collection, Peoria Public Library, Peoria, IL.

for its call letters. That story has been disputed as just coincidence, a lucky random pick. But even today, it comes up, quite frequently, as if it was willed to be true. Most people couldn't care less if it's fact or fiction. It sounds good, and it keeps the legend of Roosevelt's words alive. *Do you know what WMBD stands for?*

Roosevelt, as it turned out, had no problem adding a blurb to history when he saw something that moved him. This was, after all, a man who capitalized the word Nature, so his interests were in the beauty of the landscape and the land he fought so hard to protect. In 1911, he dubbed the 44-mile-long scenic stretch of gravel road through Arizona's canyons, cliffs, mesas, and forests "one of the most spectacular, best worth-seeing sights in the world." And as for Yellowstone, one of his favorites, he proclaimed it to be "the most beautiful place in the world!"

His words about Grand View Drive seemed to fit the pattern.

IN 1912, Roosevelt entered the presidential race and was in it to win it. The contest for a spot on the Republican ticket was a battle between Roosevelt, Taft, and Wisconsin Senator Robert LaFollete, who perhaps was even more progressive than Roosevelt. LaFollete had the momentum early on. In March, the start of the primary

season, hoping for a win in North Dakota, Roosevelt was defeated by LaFollete 58 to 39 percent. Taft got a paltry three percent. But LaFollete was not Roosevelt's worry. The incumbent's time would come, and Roosevelt knew it. A week later came the former president's most humiliating defeat as a candidate. Taft soundly beat Roosevelt in his home state of New York. Roosevelt was shocked. Crowds were huge for "Teddy" wherever he went, but the numbers didn't bear it out. Roosevelt was convinced the election was stolen after discovering some ballots arrived at polling places too late to be counted or were so badly damaged that they were unreadable. The colonel fumed and protested, but he carried on. Illinois was next. On April 9, Roosevelt won Illinois and changed the campaign. He picked up every district in the state but one. "We slugged them over the ropes," he declared on a train to the East Coast, ready for the next round. Picking up steam, Roosevelt began winning more states and in May, a stunner, an easy victory in Ohio, Taft's own state.

In mid-June, Roosevelt went to Chicago and the Republican National Convention with a majority of the states in his pocket—except for the Deep South—and strong popular support.

"The people have spoken," he said defiantly and confidently.

He lost.

Taft's machine was too big, and the state primaries, as it turned out, were just for show. In the end, hand-picked delegates at the convention decided the candidate, and Taft had more influential cronies on his side than Roosevelt. Roosevelt would enter the general election as a third-party candidate on the Progressive ticket, or "Bull Moose Party," as he called it. But it was too late. The split in the Republican Party allowed Democrat Woodrow Wilson to easily win the presidency.

Roosevelt sucked it up and did what he did best: he went exploring. In 1913, he embarked on a new adventure, traversing the elusive River of Doubt, a then-uncharted tributary of the Amazon River, now known as Roosevelt's River, or Rio Roosevelt. A year later he returned home weary and broken. The trip had done great damage physically.

In the summer of 1916, Roosevelt's friend Archbishop Spalding died in his sleep at his home in Peoria. "Why is the bell tolling?" the calls came to St. Mary's Cathedral that late afternoon. "The Archbishop is dead," was the reply. Roosevelt did not attend the funeral, a lavish affair that included many government and religious leaders from the state.

In stark contrast, on August 25, the same day of Spalding's death, President Wilson signed the act that created the National Park Service.

Roosevelt made it back to Peoria only once after his visit in 1910, in September 1914, during a two-day sweep through Illinois stumping for a Progressive party candidate for the U.S. Senate named Raymond Robbins. Roosevelt addressed a rousing audience on the steps of the Peoria County Courthouse.

When the 1916 election presidential candidates were being decided, the Progressives wanted "Teddy" back, but Roosevelt refused the nomination, instead backing the Republican candidate and his old party. Although still critical of President Wilson's foreign policies, Roosevelt wholly supported America's entry into the Great War and asked to participate, but Wilson refused. Instead he watched from the sidelines as all four of his sons served. Only three came home. In July of 1918, his youngest boy, Quentin, a pilot, was killed in an aerial attack over France.

Thanks to a surge in popularity and due in part to his passionate stance on the war, Roosevelt had aspirations for a run at the Republican nomination for president in 1920. But that ended on January 6, 1919. That day at his beloved estate on Sagamore Hill, at the age of 60, Theodore Roosevelt died. A blood clot in his lung took him quickly, and silently, while he slept.

GRAND VIEW Drive and its adjacent parks continue to be an institution in the Peoria area. In 1996, it was added to the National Register of Historic Places as a historic district. It's still owned by the Park District, and the bluff side is still underdeveloped, used for viewing only. Beyond the river bluff, elaborate homes and mansions tucked elusively behind finely coiffed rows of bushes and trees are just as interesting to scout as the scenery on the other side, giving the roadway a beauty and grandeur on many levels now.

An October stroll or drive on Grand View Drive is an annual rite of the fall season for many, and its view is just as impressive to this day as when the former president admired it many years ago.

How can anyone visit the area and not think of Roosevelt and that Columbus Day 1910 when he came to town to honor an old friend, talk politics, and take a ride in a Glide up the hill? Roosevelt may not have been the first to notice, but he certainly was moved enough by what he witnessed to inadvertently give the city a lasting tribute.

"Great. That's fine," he exclaimed, taking it all in.

Then as legend has it, he said these immortal words: "I have traveled all over the world, and this is the world's most beautiful drive."

The World's Most Beautiful Drive!

Imagine that.

SOURCE NOTES

An Affectionate Farewell

Among the plethora of Abraham Lincoln books available for research, the one I kept referring to for a broader perspective of Lincoln's days as a presidential candidate is *1861: A Civil War Awakening* by Adam Goodheart (Knopf, 2011). For information and descriptions of the Peoria Speech, there are many good sources including *Abraham Lincoln in Peoria, Illinois* by B.C. (Byron Cloyd) Bryner, 1849-1926 (Lincoln Historical Publishing Co., 1924), which also reprinted the drawing on page 8; *Lincoln at Peoria: the Turning Point: Getting Right with the Declaration of Independence* by Lewis Lehrman (Stackpole Books, 2001); *Abraham Lincoln sees Peoria: an Historical and Pictorial Record of Seventeen Visits from 1832 to 1858* by Ernest E. East (Ernest Edward), 1885-1960 (Record Pub. Co., 1939). James L. Swanson's two Lincoln books, *Manhunt: The 12-Day Chase for Lincoln's Killer* (William Morrow, 2006) and *Bloody Crimes: The Funeral of Abraham Lincoln and the Manhunt for Jefferson Davis* (William Morrow, 2010) were used for clarification on the funeral train and detective Alan Pinkerton. The description of Lincoln the night he won the presidency is from Carl Sandberg's *Lincoln: The Prairie and War Years* (Dell Pub. Co., 1969). The story of Lincoln's literary bureau was told by Dr. Samuel Melvin Houston in 1898. His account is said to have been written "while he was dying." It begins: "(In) MEMORANDUM OF CERTAIN FACTS FOR INFORMATION OF THOSE WHO FOLLOW AFTER." There are several instances of Lincoln's bureaus or chests filled with personal belongings and writings he left behind in Springfield. Houston's story was the most personal and a first-hand account. A full text of Lincoln's Peoria Speech can be found at archive.org/details/abrahamlincolnsolinc. A text of Stephen Douglas's speech in Peoria does not exist. He did not transcribe it.

Bury the Hatchet

There are several books about Jim Fisk, but only one about Edward Stokes, Fisk, Josie Mansfield and the love triangle that eventually led to Fisk's demise, *The Murder of Jim Fisk for the Love of Josie Mansfield: A Tragedy of the Gilded Age* by H.W. Brands (Anchor Books, 2011). Most of the information on Fisk's death came from this book. Also helpful was a story found online titled "Meet Edward, the Most Notorious Member of the Stokes Family." I'm not sure who else in the Stokes family might have been notorious, but its information was recopied from a newspaper article titled "Edward S. Stokes: a Sad and Shameful

Career" that appeared in the *Franklin County (Mass) Gazette* in January 1873. Stokes' long obituary in *The Sun* (New York) on November 3, 1901 is written like a book and contains chapter titles like "Fisk had Stokes Watched" and "Mansfield Held up to Ridicule." It was an invaluable resource and quite entertaining too. The history of the *Nymphs and Satyr* painting and artist William Bouguereau's life is found in a short article titled "Biography of Bouguereau's *Nymphs and Satyr*" written by David S. Brooks. I also found a *Time* magazine article dated January 25, 1943, which chronicled the painting's rebirth in New York and information on Bouguereau's death in 1905. Carrie Nation's life is well-documented by others and not surprisingly, by herself. The books I used include *Carry A. Nation: Retelling a Life* by Fran Grace (Indiana University Press, 2001), *Carry Nation* by Herbert Asbury (A.A. Knopf, 1929) and quotes found in sources from Nation's own autobiography, which were mostly reprinted in other books. (Note: I used the traditional spelling of her first name, Carrie, within the story). The outline of Nation's visit to Peoria was culled from local newspapers. The biography of Peter Weast is derived from several Peoria County history books and articles found in the Peoria Public Library history room. Bits about prohibition and Nation's quotes on drinking were found in *Last Call: The Rise and Fall of Prohibition* by David Okrent (Scribner, 2010). The history of the duplicate painting in Peoria came from newspapers, various articles, and the Peoria Historical Society.

A COLONEL FOR THE OCCASION

Trying to summarize what happened to General George Armstrong Custer and the troops at Little Bighorn is no easy task. "Summarize" is the key word here, and the challenge too. Many so-called experts have analyzed it, some quite well, some not. Perhaps the greatest narrative of Custer's life and career is *Son of the Morning Star* by Evan S. Connell (First Harper, 1991), a must read. Its detail is unmatched. Other more recent books I used include *A Terrible Glory: Custer and the Little Bighorn, The Last Great Battle of the American West* by James Donovan (Little Brown and Company, 2008) and *The Last Stand: Custer, Sitting Bull, and the Battle of the Little Bighorn* by Nathaniel Philbrick (Viking Penguin, 2010). The information on the year 1876, the National Centennial celebrations, and the elections came from *Centennial Crisis: The Disputed Election of 1876* by William H. Rehnquist (Vintage, 2007) and *The Year of the Century: 1876* by Dee Brown (Scribner, 1966). Local descriptions of the Peoria Centennial parade, including Ingersoll's speech, were from Peoria newspapers. The first-hand description of the Philadelphia Exhibition by a Peoria native was written exclusively for the *Peoria Daily-Transcript*. Robert Ingersoll's work is well documented from his writings, letters and speeches. His biographies, which are numerous, range from high praise and adulation (especially by those who knew him well) to detailed studies of the man's politics and ideologies, specifically, but not limited to, his views on religion. Ingersoll was a fascinating figure and left behind a trove of speeches and writings that are still praised and debated today. Many books on Ingersoll can be found in the history room of the Peoria Public Library's Main Campus. In this chapter, however, when it came to Ingersoll, the man, I stuck to more formal retellings: *Robert A. Ingersoll: A Life* by Frank Smith (Prometheus Books, 1990), *Colonel Bob Ingersoll: a biographical narrative of a Great American Orator and Agnostic* by Cameron Rogers (Doubleday & Page, 1927), and *American Infidel: Robert G. Ingersoll, a biography* by Orvin Larson (Citadel Press, 1962). Descriptions of Peoria life in 1876 were found in newspapers, magazines and articles.

Church Build in a Day

Nearly all the accounts of Memorial Day 1910 in Peoria and the church building are from local Peoria papers. The *Peoria Journal-Transcript* covered it well, even chronicling the event with pictures showing the building progress with photos at various points during the day. Sadly the paper's condition, and therefore the photos, was too worn in microfilm to reproduce here. While researching the West Bluff Chapel building online I was directed to an online edition of *Popular Mechanics* from 1910. The story of the church on Main Street was praised as much for its impressive feat of engineering as it was for its speed. Some passages in the story were taken from this brief article: "Popular Mechanics: An Illustrated Weekly Review" (Volume 14, issues 1-6, September 1910). The first paragraph of the article begins quite eloquently: "When a wooden building is to be erected in a newly settled country, a building bee is arranged; the neighbors from miles around gather on a certain day, and before evening the framing, walls and roof are up." The life of Ashley J. Elliott was told mostly through his obituary. His quotes on railroad demurrage were taken from "Car Efficiencies, Deficiencies: An address to Central Association of Railroad Officer, Annual Meeting, Peoria, Ill., October 16, 1908," by Ashley J. Elliott (publisher unknown, 1908). The history of Decoration Day or Memorial Day can be found in many articles online and in numerous biographies of General Ulysses S. Grant, James Garfield and General John A. Logan. Mary Logan's remembrances are found in her own book, *Reminiscences of a Soldier's Wife*, by Mrs. John A. Logan (Charles Scribner & Sons, 1913). Her recollections of visiting Civil War gravesites and suggesting a day of remembrance for the dead are revealing and personal. I used several passages in the story. The full text of the book can be found and read online. Finally, the accounts of October 11, 1866 in Peoria were from newspapers and an essay by Peoria historian Norman V. Kelly titled "The Shaft."

Stand-Up Statesmen

Usher Linder's name is best known in Coles County, Illinois, specifically Charleston, where he lived and worked. Several websites cover the history of Coles County. Still, there's not a lot about Linder. I used his own book, *Reminiscences of the Early Bench and Bar* by General Usher F. Linder (The Chicago Legal News Co., 1879), although it is not an

autobiography. Instead, the book includes biographical sketches of the
men, mostly lawyers or judges, he worked alongside or admired, including Lincoln. The introduction of the book, however, is about Linder,
the man, written with great affection by a friend, another lawyer, John
Gillespie. Most of the passages and anecdotes about Linder's life and
law career come from this account. Linder's first meeting with Abraham Lincoln is in Linder's own words. Another invaluable resource
was *Usher F. Linder: Orator from Coles* by Roma Linder Bradley (Indiana University Press, 1965) written in 1963. Lincoln's time as a lawyer
is well-documented by several books including *Lincoln the Lawyer*, by
Brian Dirck (University of Illinois Press, 2007) to which I referred the
most. Several of Lincoln's court stories were found in *Abe Lincoln's
Yarns and Stories* by Alexander K. McClure (The John C. Winston Co.,
1969) and *The Wit and Wisdom of Abraham Lincoln*, edited by Anthony
Gross (Fall River Press, 1994). The trial of the steamboat *Effie Afton*
is from *Hell Gate of the Mississippi: The Effie Afton Trial and Abraham Lincoln's Role in It*, by Larry A. Rinney (Talesman Press, 2007).
Other references to Lincoln were found in *Herndon's Lincoln: The Story of a Great Life* by William Herndon (The Herndon Lincoln Publishing Company, 1888) and *Inside Lincoln's White House: The Complete Civil War Diary of John Hay* by Michael Burlingame (Southern
Illinois University Press, 1999). Descriptions of Lincoln's appearance
are from Carl Sandberg's *Lincoln: The Prairie and War Years* (Dell,
1969). The examination of Lincoln's humor is from the appropriately titled essay "Lincoln's Humor: An Analysis," by Benjamin P. Thomas *(Journal of the Abraham Lincoln Association*, Vol. 3, No. 1, 1981).
Many quotes from colleagues of Lincoln's about his humor are from
this extensive and thought-provoking read. The story of the Metamora
murder trial is from an essay by Ernest E. East titled "Lincolniana:
The Melissa Goings Murder Case," *(Journal of the Illinois State Historical Society*, Vol. 46, No. 1, 1953). East was a newspaperman and
columnist from Peoria. His writings and correspondence letters are
now part of a collection called "The Ernest Edward East Papers, 1934-
1960" at the Abraham Lincoln Presidential Museum and Library in
Springfield. Also helpful is an essay by Jean Meyer titled "Justice Served:
Abraham Lincoln and the Melissa Goings Case" *(Art & Society* magazine, March/April 2009). The history of Metamora, Illinois is from
the *Metamora Sentinel* and various articles.

A PLOTTER'S TALE

As I mention in the story, thanks to writer Bill Moon, we have a detailed
account of the first murder trial ever recorded in Peoria County. I give
Moon credit because many years ago, in 1912, he actually went to the
circuit court and found the old records (even back then it was old).
Moon was able to cover it well, and I found his versions of events being
copied in other works like *The Boundaries Between Us: Natives and
Newcomers along the Frontier of the Old Northwest Territories, 1750 to
1850*, edited by Daniel Barr (Kent State University Press, Ohio, 2006),

a collection of essays on Native Americans in the Old Northwest. In the essay "Negotiating Law on the Frontier: Responses to Cross-Cultural Homicide in Illinois 1810-1825," written by Bruce C. Smith, Barr notes in his introduction that Smith "examines the seldom addressed ways in which Americans and natives peoples engaged the law in response to the murder of one of their own by another." Conceding that there is "scant extent scholarship devoted to the study of murder in the Old Northwest territory," Smith sources Moon's work and mentions the Illinois State Archives in Springfield as having the case records on file. Moon's full story is titled "The Story of No-Ma-Que: Court Records Tell An Interesting Story of Peoria County's First Murder Trial" and was first published by the *Journal of the Illinois State Historical Society* in 1912. The story of William Hamilton before and after the Nomaque trial is from *Alexander's Pioneer Son: The Life and Times of Colonel William Stephen Hamilton 1797-1850. Early New York, Missouri, Illinois, Michigan, Wisconsin, Iowa and California* by Sylvan Joseph Muldoon (Aurand Press, 1930). I give a brief snapshot of author Muldoon in the story because without his work, Hamilton's exploits might have been lost to time. Muldoon's interest in Hamilton, I suppose, could only be explained by his being a native of Wisconsin and not in his particular area of expertise, which was metaphysical science. I could find no connection between the two. For Hamilton's time in Wisconsin and "The Diggings," I found several good essays online including "Billy Hamilton and the Hamilton Diggings, now known as Wiota" (author not listed), found on the website of the Lafayette County (Wisconsin) Historical Society. For information on Alexander Hamilton, Aaron Burr and the infamous duel, I referenced *Alexander Hamilton* by Ron Chernow (Penguin, 2004). For the history of Green Bay, Wisconsin, I used an article titled "Origins of French and English Names for the Bay of Green Bay" by Clifford E. Kraft from the book *Voyageur, Historical Review of Brown County and Northeast Wisconsin* (Brown County Historical Society, 1984). The history of early Peoria is found in *The History of Peoria County* (Johnson and Company, Chicago, 1880). Jacques Marquette quotes are found in *Father Marquette's Journal* by Jacques Marquette (complied and published by the Michigan Historical Center, 1998). Although I love maps, the location of streets in Peoria is personally recalled.

A Peoria Love Story

There is no shortage of good and informative books on old-time radio programs. The internet is also a great archive. With the click of a mouse you can listen to just about any episode of any popular program from the medium's early days. The information I used for the *Vic and Sade Show* is *The Vic and Sade Story* by Bill Idelson (BearManorMedia, 2012). The book is filled mostly with scripts from the *Vic and Sade Show*, as the writing clearly took center stage. Idleson includes a biographical sketch on Paul Rhymer and his inspiration for the show, which I used in my story. The best source on Jim and Marian Jordan is *Heaven-*

ly Days: The Story of Fibber McGee and Molly by Charles Stumpf and Tom Price (World of Yesterday, 1987). Most of the information on their time in radio is from this book. Sadly it is out of print, but several copies can be found in the Peoria Public Library. As mentioned in the story, an extensive interview with Jim Jordan was conducted by Wally Gair in 1984, four years before Jordan's death. A portion of the interview was transcribed. The full audio is in The University of Illinois, Springfield, Norris L. Brookens Library Archives/Special Collections titled "Jim Jordan Memoir" and is described as follows: "Jordan, native of Peoria, discusses his career in radio. He recalls the town of Peoria around the turn of the century, the development of his character 'Fibber McGee' on the radio show *Fibber McGee and Molly*, network radio, and radio personalities." Most of the information about the Jordans in Peoria, the war years, and their rise in show business is from this interview. The history of the stock market crash of 1929 and the subsequent Great Depression is from several sources, including *Rainbows End: The Crash of 1929* by Maury Klein (Oxford University Press, 2001) and *Six Days in October: The Stock Market Crash of 1929* (Wall Street Journal Book/ Atheneum Books, 2002). The story of the Jordan's return visit to Peoria is from the Peoria newspapers and *Look* magazine (April 25, 1950, Vol. 14 No. 9). There is some misinformation on when the Jordans actually came back to Peoria, specifically which month. Most sources claim they were in Peoria in April 1950, the month the *Look* article was published. But they actually visited in February of that year. The papers confirmed it. Thankfully, I was able to find a copy of the *Look* magazine edition featuring "Fibber McGee and Molly" on eBay. I don't know how I could have done the story without it. My original copy is a little frayed on the edges and turning brown in color, but it's a treasure trove of historical information for the 1950s. The Fibber McGee and Molly article is quite humorous and fun. "Lots of people wanted to see what became of that Jordan boy," the article proclaims. Unfortunately, I could not include all the wonderful photos from the magazine in the book. Jim and Marian Jordan's special night as honorees at Bradley University was covered through the *Look* article and newspapers.

GUARD THE MAIL

A. Scott Beg wrote the definitive book on the life of Charles A. Lindbergh, simply titled, *Lindbergh* (G.P. Putnam's Sons, 1998). It is an exhaustive look at the man, meticulously researched, and a good read to boot, all 640 pages of it. Lindbergh was a fascinating figure in American history. His rise to fame was quick, and his fall from grace was just as sudden, but his record flight is still held in high regard. He seemed to enjoy being Charles Lindbergh best before the spotlight shined on him so brightly, when he was flying planes for show and carrying the mail through the air over Illinois (although he admitted it was a difficult job). There are many stories about Lindbergh in Peoria and surrounding towns, mostly stopover visits during mail runs (I'm not sure he ever came here by car). The story of Lindbergh's commemorative

mail run is told through the Peoria newspapers. I didn't find much else
of it in other people's books, even Berg's. There were important events
in Lindbergh's schedule around that time, and the two days he took to
fly the mail again across Illinois apparently wasn't one of them. Regardless, the local papers covered it well, and it truly was a national event
since people from all over the country wanted a letter on that plane. I've
seen Lindbergh postcards marked from both coasts and everywhere in-
between. The story of the ditched flight over Peoria before he became
famous is taken from several accounts: Lindbergh himself in *"WE"*
The Famous Flyer's own Story of his Life and his Transatlantic Flight,
Together with his Views on the Future of Aviation by Charles A. Lindbergh (Grossett and Dunlap, 1927), Berg's book, *Lindbergh,* and *Atlantic Fever Lindbergh, His Competitors and the Race to Cross the Atlantic*
by Joe Jackson (Farrar, Straus Giroux, 2012). In addition, I relied on
newspaper coverage from Peoria and Bloomington, Illinois' *The Daily
Pantagraph.* A first-hand account of the wreck is recalled from Pete
Thompson, the farmer who helped Lindbergh find the plane and Lindbergh himself, who wrote about the wreck for the *Aeronautic Review*
in the November 1, 1936 issue, the article titled, "He Does it Again,"
by Charles A. Lindbergh. The history of the U.S. Air Mail comes from
many good sources including *Mavericks of the Sky: The First Daring
Pilots of the U.S. Air Mail* by Barry Rosenburg and Catherine Macaulay
(HarperCollins, 2006), *Flying the Mail* by Donald Dale Jackson (Time-
Life Books, 1982), *Tracks Across the Sky: the Story of the Pioneers of the
U.S. Air Mail* by Page Shamburger (J.B. Lippincott Co., 1964), and *The
Airmail: Jennies to Jets* by Benjamin B. Lipsner (Wilcox & Follett Com-
pany, 1951). Captain Lipsner's first-hand account of being on the tar-
mac for the inaugural mail run was a great source, and find. The book
is out of print. Many of the stories and quotes from the early airmail
pilots come from these sources. The Wright Brothers story is from *First
Flight: the Wright Brothers and the Invention of the Airplane* by T.A.
Heppenheimer (John Wiley & Sons, 2003) and *Wilbur and Orville: A
Biography of the Wright Brothers* by Fred Howard (Knopf, 1987).

A MOTOR BUG'S DELIGHT

Theodore Roosevelt's visit to Peoria on Columbus Day, 1910 was front-
page, headline news, not just locally but nationally. The *Peoria Daily Journal* covered it well from a local perspective. Both the *New York
Times* and the *New York-Tribune* covered the events in Peoria and in
St. Louis the day before. The sketch of pilot Archibald Hoxsey is tak-
en from newspaper accounts and the Wright Brothers books previously mentioned. Information on Archbishop Spalding is from *The Life of
John Lancaster Spalding: The First Bishop of Peoria* by David Francis
Sweeney (Herder and Herder, 1965). The description of the Glide is
from newspaper ads. The history of cross-country treks by automobile is
found in *Coast to Coast by Automobile: The Pioneering Trips 1899-1908*
by Curt McConnell (Stanford University Press, 2000). I used this book
for the Davis' trip and all the other attempts at transcontinental travel

noted in the story except for the Gehrs. For the Gehrs' story, I went
to the newspapers. The Gehrs' time in Peoria was well reported and
included snippets about their journey up to that point. The New York
papers in December 1907 provided coverage the rest of the way. McConnell does touch on the apparent deception of the car being steamed to
New York instead of driven and confirms it with a reference from Mrs.
Gehr's diary. The original diary still exists today, and is quite brittle, I
might add, at the Wheels O' Time Museum in Dunlap, Illinois, just
north of Peoria. For background on Theodore Roosevelt and the elections of 1912 and 1916, I used several informative Roosevelt biographies,
including *Colonel Roosevelt* by Edmund Morris (Random House, 2010),
*The Bully Pulpit: Theodore Roosevelt, William Howard Taft, and the
Golden Age of Journalism* by Doris Kearns Goodwin (Simon and Schus-
ter, 2013), *River of Doubt* by Candace Millard (Doubleday, 2005) and
*Theodore Roosevelt: The American Presidents Series: The 26TH President
1901-1909* by Louis Auchincloss (Times Books, 2002). The history of
Grand View Drive is from these sources: *Peoria Heights, Illinois, Keeping Pace with Progress: Diamond Jubilee 1898-1973* (Peoria Heights
Diamond Jubilee Committee, Historical Booklet, 1973), the Peoria
newspapers, and *The Peorian,* a business and industrial magazine from
the early 1900s. Many issues of *The Peorian* are still on file and are available to view in the Peoria Public Library history room. Descriptions of
the scenic wonder that is Grand View Drive both yesterday and today
are from *A History of Peoria County* and my own personal reflections.
Roosevelt was right. It truly is a most beautiful drive.

ACKNOWLEDGEMENTS

THERE ARE many people to thank in the making of *Peoria Stories*. First, I owe my deepest gratitude to the team at Amika Press: Dr. Jay Amberg for his belief in this project and encouragement along the way; Sarah Koz for her terrific design work and attention to detail; and editor John Manos whose advice, suggestions and general knowledge of what makes a good story challenged me to be a better writer. It was his insistence early on that I take my time with this book. For that, I'm truly grateful.

A very gracious thanks goes to the staff at the Peoria Public Library, the Morton Public Library, the Peoria Historical Society, Gary Bragg of the Wheels O' Time Museum, The Sacramento City Cemetery, the Abraham Lincoln Presidential Museum and Library, and the Library of Congress for their help in research.

Personal thanks, in no particular order, goes to Paul Gordon and Kevin Kizer of *The Peorian*, Mike Wild of *Alpha Media*, Norman Kelly, Connie and David Perkins, Bob Killion, Christophe Traugott, Greg Batton, Rick McDermott, Randy Whalen, Michael Zurski and my extended family.

Finally, a special thank you goes to my wife Connie for her unwavering support. She is my go-to person for everything. Her advice and recommendations led to spirited discussions and decisions which made this book better. I couldn't have done it without her. Sam and Nora make my day, every day.

ABOUT THE AUTHOR

KEN ZURSKI is a longtime broadcaster and author of *The Wreck of the Columbia*. A native of Chicagoland, where he was a radio personality for many years, Ken now works in Peoria and resides in Morton with his wife Connie and two children, Sam and Nora. *Peoria Stories* is his second book.

CONNECT WITH Ken online at facebook.com/kenzurskiauthor

ABOUT THE AUTHOR

www.ingramcontent.com/pod-product-compliance
Lightning Source LLC
Chambersburg PA
CBHW070350090426
42733CB00009B/1357